T0083812

"Culture" and Culture

"Culture" and Culture:
Traditional Knowledge and Intellectual Rights

Manuela Carneiro da Cunha

PRICKLY PARADIGM PRESS
CHICAGO

Prickly Paradigm Press, LLC
5629 South University Avenue
Chicago, Il 60637

www.prickly-paradigm.com

ISBN-10: 0-9761475-6-4
ISBN-13: 978-0-9761475-6-5
LCCN: 2009936908

Printed in the United States of America on acid-free paper.

Cantes de Ida y Vuelta

Cantes de ida y vuelta, such as guajiras, colombianas and milongas, have been traditional genres in Andalusian flamenco since at least the nineteenth century—the century that inaugurated the postcolonial era for the Spanish empire. As Spain was exiting colonialism, most other Western countries were entering it. But then Spain had always been ahead of the times. Cantes de ida y vuelta, which translates as something like "round trip flamenco songs" were colonial products: the result of the appropriation and transformation in colonies such as Cuba, Colombia and Argentina (as they are now known), and their subsequent re-introduction in Spain. Hence the round trip.

Postcoloniality is not merely the predicament of former colonies: it is also in a major way a predicament of former colonial powers. Metropoles of old must now come to terms with the tide of once imperial subjects moving in on them. Analytical categories—I am avoiding the loftier word "concepts"—that were manufactured in the core and were exported and applied to the rest of the world are also moving back to haunt their producers: as with *flamenco cantes*, they too are round trip things, diffracted and returned to sender. *Ida y vuelta* categories.

One such category is "culture." Race, and later culture, along with such other notions as work, money and hygiene, were all exported goods (or evils). People in the periphery of the world core were supposed to buy into them no less than they were expected to buy manufactured commodities. While some of these ideas, as Jean and John Comaroff have shown, were largely spread by missionaries in the nineteenth century, one might well argue that anthropologists were the main purveyors of the idea of "culture" in the twentieth century. Anthropologists largely carried the outgoing trip of "culture" in their wings. Since then and up to this very day, "culture" is being endorsed and refurbished in the periphery. As Terry Turner first pointed out, it is proving to be a major argument in all sorts of land and other claims.

There are further parallels with the unexpected itineraries of other categories. Christianity was exported from the West as a colonial product and was imposed onto a large part of Africa. Yet, somewhat paradoxically, it fell to African Christianity to play a major role in challenging colonial powers. Likewise, "culture," once introduced all over the world, is having an unprecedented role as a political wedge, a "weapon of the weak" as James Scott might say. Nowhere is this more clear than in the debates surrounding traditional peoples' intellectual rights. This is not simply because knowledge is the first item listed in Edward Tylor's definition of culture. Rather, it is because issues of intellectual rights have revived debates about culture in major ways.

There are significant differences in the comparison between Christianity and "culture." For all the sixteenth-century discussion of New World people being the lost tribes of Israel, peripheral peoples were not supposed to have known true religion before it was handed down to them by colonial powers and the Church. "Culture" is somewhat trickier, since "culture" is what these people were supposed to have had all along. In Marxian language, it is as if they had "'culture' in itself" even as they might not have had "'culture' for themselves." Be that as it may, there is no doubt that most of them have acquired the latter sort of "culture," the one "for themselves" that they can now pose against the rest of the world. To be sure, this is a double-edged sword, since it constrains its bearers ostensibly to perform "their culture."

I am a firm believer in the existence of internalized coherence schemata that organize people's perception and action and allow for some degree of communication in social groups, something along the lines of what has been called culture by anthropologists. Equally, I believe that the latter does not coincide with "culture" as it has been taken up by various peoples, and that there are significant disparities between the two. This is not to say that the content of culture will necessarily differ from that of "culture;" rather that they are not in the same universe of discourse, which is of some consequence. In sum, I will be arguing that this is a particularly deceptive case of "false friendship": and as quotation marks are not always perceptible, culture and "culture" get mixed up.

This is the kind of round trip I was referring to. It has been somewhat embarrassing to some anthropologists that they should discard the category of culture for largely political considerations right at the time when people out there are using cultural rights (and quite successfully so) for redressing political wrongs. Culture seems to be coming back with a vengeance to haunt Western theory.

The adventures of "culture" do not stop here. If culture and "culture" are at odds with each other, an interesting problem arises that begs ethnographic research: what are the processes, the issues and the transformations entailed in the adjustment and translation of the imported category of "culture" by peripheral people? If I may borrow a term and a fruitful idea from Marshall Sahlins, the question becomes: how is the indigenization of "culture" achieved?

A First Story

The massive old man stood up. With a fierce countenance, looking down at the audience, he spoke in an indignant voice and in rough Portuguese: "Does someone here hold that *honi* is *cultura* [culture]? I say: no, it is not! *Honi* is not *cultura*!"

Now, you have to understand that we were discussing indigenous intellectual rights in cultural items, and more specifically rights on the use of a frog secretion—an entirely different matter from *honi*—yet everyone understood why the old Yawanawa leader brought it up. As this is a rather long story, I'll only let you know at this stage that *honi* is the Yawanawa word for a hallucinogenic beverage, based on a combination of two different plants, and widely known under different names—*ayahuasca*, *yagé*, *kaapi*—in the Western Amazonian basin. By the late seventies *ayahuasca* or *honi* had been incorporated into a set of different non-indigenous popular urban religions in the Amazonian state of Acre. In the eighties and nineties, these religions met with great success in major centers in Southeastern Brazil, including Rio de Janeiro and São Paulo, among ecologically-minded intellectuals, TV actors, new age youth and, interestingly, former guerrilla leaders. Eventually, starting in the nineties, some of these religions were exported to the US and to Europe. I will return to this topic below.

Back to the scene of the old Yananawa man's indignation. It was in June, 2005, on the second day of an elaborate meeting in Rio Branco, the capital of Acre, that brought together several different ethnic groups from the state and from the southwest of the state of the Amazon. The first day had been given to long explanations by a lawyer from the Ministry of the Environment about the legal framework for claiming intellectual rights in traditional knowledge. The next day, several indigenous peoples engaged in a debate on how to share the possible benefits among themselves. The meeting was linked to the issue that had arisen two years earlier. It concerned intellectual rights in the knowledge of the use of the above-mentioned frog secretion, a story that will be told in detail later in this pamphlet. The Katukina, Yawanawa, Kaxinawa, and all the other interfluvial indigenous Panoan language speakers, in both Brazil and Peru, plus some of their neighbors, could claim the same traditional knowledge. Yet only the forceful Yawanawa, as well as some Kaxinawa and Katukina, were present. On the other hand, some Apurinã, who had no claims to that frog knowledge, had stayed on to watch the debate, looking rather puzzled with the discussion but also suddenly awakened to new possibilities. The major Ashaninka personality, Francisco Pyianko, State Secretary for Indigenous People, was also there. His demeanor and influence, along with the fact that he had from the start withdrawn any possible claim by the Ashaninka to knowledge of the secretion, gave him great moral authority. Although Arawak-speaking Ashaninka eventually used the frog secretion, they had, he asserted, learnt it from their Panoan-speaking neighbors.

The objective of the meeting was to reach some consensus on how to go ahead legitimately with negotiations on knowledge of the use of the frog secretion. The Katukina were the originators of the whole business, and had been able to enlist the Ministry of the Environment's support, as will be explained below. In this assembly, however, the three Katukina present were cornered into an uncomfortable position, with Yawanawa and to a lesser extent Kaxinawa people accusing them of wanting to monopolize knowledge that was common to everyone present. Yawanawa share titled indigenous land with the Katukina, a *sui generis* arrangement with a real potential for conflict. Due to their history of breaking ties with protestant missionaires and establishing business alliances with such North American firms as Aveda, the Yawanawa tend to be far more savvy than the Katukina in all matters urban, as well as in external international links.

In a sense, they had at one point come to consider Katukina as their own local sample of traditional people. In the capital city of the state, where this meeting was taking place, Yawanawa accordingly largely outnumbered and rhetorically dominated the small Katukina delegation. But there was some irony in the situation, since the "primitive" Katukina had taken the lead in this matter.

To understand what was going on and to be able to unpack the event, much more context is needed. The context here covers, as it often should, different areas arranged in order of magnitude. I'll have to unravel international legal instruments, transnational interest groups, national, subnational and local policies, indigenous politics, scientific politics—probably much more than one wishes to know. But each area needs to be elucidated to understand the whole context.

Next, I will have to tell a detective story of sorts: the story of the frog, with a full cast of characters.

Why should I presume there is any interest in any of this? Well, for one, this is an ethnography of novel events that have equivalents in many parts of the world, having emerged in this guise around the mid-1990s.

My own interest is as follows. First, I think that we lack chronicles these days. Contemporary historians of, say, the nineteenth century rely a great deal on the stories travelers produced. Those stories were a genre in themselves. They chronicled events and atmospheres that were too minute to claim a place in the news, and too taken for granted to be worthy of any public registry. Intimate journals were for sentiments and unusual events. Only travelers could deem as interesting or even striking that which otherwise went without saying. Not that they did it without a heavy bias and badly tuned ear. Yet, in this era of representational reflexivity and angst, I would like to put in a good word for travelers and naïve ethnographers. Who, I ask, is giving us a reasoned chronicle of minute events that take place in faraway sites today?

Such stories take us back to the vexed issue of culture. Not so much as an analytical anthropological category, but rather as a vernacular one. I'm interested, for example, in understanding why the old Yawanawa leader thinks *honi* is not *cultura*. But I also want to look into the relation between what anthropologists have traditionally called culture, and what indigenous people are calling "culture." I am interested not only in the logical relation between the two, but also the effects of the co-presence of those two uses/meanings of culture: does such coexistence have any effect, and does it entail consequences?

How Do Negotiations About Traditional Knowledge Arise in the First Place?

The very possibility of transactions in traditional knowledge and the requirement of formal agreements on the part of native Brazilians are grounded in a global legal and institutional construct that can be traced back to 1992 and the Convention for Biological Diversity. That legal construct, in turn, is based on assumptions of the status, nature, production and circulation of knowledge, be it "traditional" or "scientific." Further assumptions concern the kinds of rights they entail. Such assumptions and their fragility, however, are pragmatically overlooked for the sake of achieving some working (mis)understanding.

The most important consequence of the new legal construct is to define or redefine the relationship between people and knowledge. The Convention speaks about "holders," not "proprietors," of traditional knowledge. It also speaks about "sovereignty" rather than "dominion" or "proprietorship" of national states over genetic resources. Whatever the precautions taken, however, when considered pragmatically, transactions over traditional knowledge, whether they involve informed consent for research or contracts for benefit sharing, actually produce a relation approaching ownership. The possessive pronoun says it all. *Mutatis mutanda*, one could endorse what Mark Rose eloquently wrote on copyright in the seventeenth century as producing the twin birth of the concept of authorship and of the author's proprietary relations to his or her work:

> The principal institutional embodiment of the author-work relation is copyright which... by endowing it with legal reality, produces and affirms the very identity of the author... We here observe... the simultaneous emergence in the discourse of the law of the proprietary author and the literary work. The two concepts are bound to each other.

If the June 2005 meeting in Rio Branco is any indication, the concept of ownership in knowledge has been seized by indigenous people in the course of their interface with Western society—and actually taken to new heights. Someone in the audience, for example, brought up the issue of "language": *What business do these missionaries and anthropologists have in learning 'our' language? Up to now, we have naively taught it to them. But what kind of use are they putting it to?"* I should add that, surreal as it seems now, this claim might have to do with the US use of the Navaho language for military intelligence in World War II.

UN Talk on Traditional Knowledge: The Brundtland Report and the Earth Summit

Official international talk on traditional knowledge of the environment can be traced back to the landmark 1987 Brundtland Report, also known as "Our Common Future: the Report of the World Commission on Environment and Development (WCED)." The Report, under the leadership of Ms. Gro Harlem Brundtland, then Norway's prime minister, was commissioned by the UN in 1983 and submitted to its General Assembly in 1989.

Paragraph 46 of the introduction to the report states:

> Tribal and indigenous peoples will need special attention as the forces of economic development threaten their life-styles—*life-styles that can offer modern societies many lessons in the management of resources in complex forest, mountain and dry-land ecosystems.* Some are threatened by virtual extinction by insensitive development over which they have no control. Their traditional rights should be recognized and they should be given a decisive voice in formulating policies about resource development in their areas. (My emphasis)

One of the institutional results of the Brundtland Report and its discussion at the UN 1989 General Assembly Meeting, was the convening of the so-called Rio Earth Summit—that is, the United Nations Conference on Environment and Development (UNCED) in Rio de Janeiro that explicitly espoused "sustainable development" as a guiding agenda. The Rio *Declaration on Environment and Development* was issued at the Summit and states in its principle 22 that "indigenous people... have a vital role in environmental management and development because of their vital knowledge and traditional practices."

So-called Agenda 21, the official report of the UNCED, details a sustainable development program for the twenty-first century. A whole long chapter, chapter 26, titled *Recognizing and Strengthening the Role of Indigenous People and Their Communities,* deals with the issue. It is worth noting that the expression "traditional scientific knowledge" of natural resources, land and environment appears in chapter 26 of Agenda 21 along with the more usual wordings such as "traditional resource management practices." This "scientific" qualification is all the more remarkable since it is absent from other documents. Hence when spelling out the basis for recognition and enlistment of indigenous and traditional people, Agenda 21 declares:

> [Indigenous people and their communities] have developed over many generations a holistic *traditional scientific knowledge* of their lands, natural resources and environment.... In view of the interrelationship between the natural environment and its sustainable development and the cultural, social, economic and physical well-being of indigenous

people, national and international efforts to implement environmentally sound and sustainable development should recognize, accommodate, promote
and strengthen the role of indigenous people and
their communities. (My emphasis)

Agenda 21 goes into recommendations of
structural and national legal conditions for ensuring
land and decision-making control, as well as intellectual
and cultural rights, and is a thorough document in
many aspects. Notably, however, and in contrast to the
Convention on Biological Diversity (on which more
later), it does not deal with benefit sharing with indigenous people:

Objectives

26.3. In full partnership with indigenous people and
their communities, Governments and, where appropriate, intergovernmental organizations should aim
at fulfilling the following objectives:

(a) Establishment of a process to empower indigenous people and their communities through measures
that include:

(i) Adoption or strengthening of appropriate
policies and/or legal instruments at the national
level;

(ii) Recognition that the lands of indigenous
people and their communities should be protected
from activities that are environmentally unsound
or that the indigenous people concerned consider
to be socially and culturally inappropriate;

(iii) Recognition of their values, traditional knowledge and resource management practices with a view to promoting environmentally sound and sustainable development;

(iv) Recognition that traditional and direct dependence on renewable resources and ecosystems, including sustainable harvesting, continues to be essential to the cultural, economic and physical well-being of indigenous people and their communities;

(v) Development and strengthening of national dispute-resolution arrangements in relation to settlement of land and resource-management concerns;

(vi) Support for alternative environmentally sound means of production to ensure a range of choices on how to improve their quality of life so that they effectively participate in sustainable development;

(vii) Enhancement of capacity-building for indigenous communities, based on the adaptation and exchange of traditional experience, knowledge and resource-management practices, to ensure their sustainable development;

(b) Establishment, where appropriate, of arrangements to strengthen the active participation of indigenous people and their communities in the national formulation of policies, laws and programs relating to resource management and other development processes that may affect them, and their initiation of proposals for such policies and programs;

(c) Involvement of indigenous people and their communities at the national and local levels in resource management and conservation strategies and other relevant programs established to support and review sustainable development strategies, such as those suggested in other programme areas of Agenda 21.

Activities

26.4. Some indigenous people and their communities may require, in accordance with national legislation, greater control over their lands, self-management of their resources, participation in development decisions affecting them, including, where appropriate, participation in the establishment or management of protected areas. The following are some of the specific measures which Governments could take:

(a) Consider the ratification and application of existing international conventions relevant to indigenous people and their communities (where not yet done) and provide support for the adoption by the General Assembly of a declaration on indigenous rights;

(b) Adopt or strengthen appropriate policies and/ or legal instruments that will protect indigenous intellectual and cultural property and the right to preserve customary and administrative systems and practices.

...

26.5. United Nations organizations and other international development and finance organizations and Governments should, drawing on the active participation of indigenous people and their communities, as appropriate, take the following measures, inter alia, to incorporate their values, views and knowledge, including the unique contribution of indigenous women, in resource management and other policies and programs that may affect them:

(a) Appoint a special focal point within each international organization, and organize annual interorganizational coordination meetings in consultation with Governments and indigenous organizations, as appropriate, and develop a procedure within and between operational agencies for assisting Governments in ensuring the coherent and coordinated incorporation of the views of indigenous people in the design and implementation of policies and programs. Under this procedure, indigenous people and their communities should be informed and consulted and allowed to participate in national decision-making, in particular regarding regional and international cooperative efforts. In addition, these policies and programs should take fully into account strategies based on local indigenous initiatives;

(b) Provide technical and financial assistance for capacity-building programs to support the sustainable self-development of indigenous people and their communities;

(c) Strengthen research and education programs aimed at:

(i) Achieving a better understanding of indigenous people's knowledge and management experience related to the environment, and applying this to contemporary development challenges;

(ii) Increasing the efficiency of indigenous people's resource management systems, for example, by promoting the adaptation and dissemination of suitable technological innovations;

(d) Contribute to the endeavours of indigenous people and their communities in resource management and conservation strategies (such as those that may be developed under appropriate projects funded through the Global Environment Facility and the Tropical Forestry Action Plan) and other programme areas of Agenda 21, including programs to collect, analyse and use data and other information in support of sustainable development projects.

26.6. Governments, in full partnership with indigenous people and their communities should, where appropriate:

(a) Develop or strengthen national arrangements to consult with indigenous people and their communities with a view to reflecting their needs and incorporating their values and traditional and other knowledge and practices in national policies and programs in the field of natural resource management and conservation and other development programs affecting them;

...

Means of implementation

...

(b) Legal and administrative frameworks

26.8. Governments should incorporate, in collaboration with the indigenous people affected, the rights and responsibilities of indigenous people and their communities in the legislation of each country, suitable to the country's specific situation. Developing countries may require technical assistance to implement these activities.

(c) Human resource development

26.9. International development agencies and Governments should commit financial and other resources to education and training for indigenous people and their communities to develop their capacities to achieve their sustainable self-development, and to contribute to and participate in sustainable and equitable development at the national level. Particular attention should be given to strengthening the role of indigenous women.

The Convention on Biological Diversity

The Convention on Biological Diversity (CBD) was also a product of the Earth Summit, and was accordingly opened for signatures in June 1992. It has since been ratified by almost 200 countries, with the notable exception of the US who, although having signed it, has declined to ratify it to this day.

The main purpose of the CBD was to regulate access to genetic resources and benefit-sharing provisions. Prior to 1992, genetic resources were deemed the common heritage of mankind. But in contrast to the free accessibility of genetic resources, intellectual property rights in inventions derived from those resources were completely privatized. Further, by a strange providence, genetic resources and patents were particularly dense in geographically distinct areas, such that technology and genetic resources occupied complementary spaces. Genetically rich countries tended to lack cutting-edge technology while the most technologically advanced countries tended to lack wealth in genetic resources. As patents were heavily concentrated in the Northern Hemisphere, such a disjunction was soon spatialized into what became known as the North-South divide—something that corresponded at the time with the divide between the G-7 (the seven richest countries) and all other countries. This was, to be sure, a *sui generis* South that ignored geographical coordinates and included China while excluding Australia.

As wealth in genetic resources and industrialization seem to be inversely proportional, it is not surprising that the South, or at least some of its sectors, have perceived the CBD as an instrument of redistributive justice. The Convention establishes sovereignty of each and every country over its own genetic resources. Its design is a trade-off through which countries allow for regulated access to their genetic resources in exchange for technology transfer and more general benefit sharing.

By the nineties, the category "South" was in full political operation in different arenas and could stand for a variety of aggregates of countries and regions. In its genetic resources version, "South" translated into a bloc of increasingly articulated mega-diverse countries—a coalition that goes by the acronym LMMC, standing for "Like-minded Mega Diverse Countries," and comprises Bolivia, Brazil, China, Colombia, Costa Rica, Popular Republic of Congo, Ecuador, India,

Indonesia, Kenya, Madagascar, Malaysia, Mexico, Peru, the Philippines, South Africa and Venezuela. That is, almost all the tropical Latin-American countries, most Southeast Asian countries, several African states and China.

This well-oiled coalition regularly opposed the holders of the vast majority of intellectual property rights—namely Japan, the European Union and of course the United States of America. As the US never ratified the CBD, it was not officially a party to the Convention, but the Canadian, Australian and even New Zealand governments were understood to repre-sent its interests.

It goes without saying that indigenous rights were never at the top of Megadiverse countries' concerns; rather, indigenous rights followed from these countries' vested interests in their genetic resources. India and Brazil took the lead in the Megadiverse coun-tries bloc from the start. Both stand out as interesting cases, as they were also at the forefront of some of the most prominent compulsory licensing actions, where public health was used to assert a right to overcome patent restrictions. Manufacturing low-cost AIDS drugs was the first such case, brought about in Brazil by the Minister of Health during the Cardoso government (1994-2002). Provision for compulsory licensing in a small number of exceptional circumstances was part of the Trade Related Intellectual Property Agreements (TRIPs). Enforcing those provisions, however, is another matter altogether. The Brazilian government has also shown an increasing tendency since 2003 to contest the rigidity of copyrights in all areas. Gilberto Gil, as the Brazilian Minister for Culture (2003-2007) and himself a world-renowned composer and singer, backed a movement to make copyrights more flexible. He promoted Creative Commons, the *à la carte* copyright system under which this very pamphlet is being published.

As for indigenous people in Brazil, the issue is more complex—as we shall see when we discuss the history of legal provisions concerning traditional knowledge.

The contribution to conservation of traditional knowledge and benefit-sharing issues comes up in the preamble (paragraph 12) and in at least two other passages of the CBD, but most strikingly in article 8, paragraph j:

> 8. [Each contracting party, as far as possible and as appropriate]
>
> (j) Subject to its national legislation, respect, preserve and maintain knowledge, innovations and practices of indigenous and local communities embodying traditional lifestyles relevant for the conservation and sustainable use of biological diversity and promote their wider application with the approval and involvement of the holders of such knowledge, innovations and practices and encourage the equitable sharing of the benefits arising from the utilization of such knowledge, innovations and practices;

It is noteworthy that where Agenda 21 speaks of intellectual and cultural rights, no doubt a source of material and moral entitlements, the CBD speaks in more general terms of equitable benefit sharing. Further, indigenous and local communities are paired in article 8j whereas Agenda 21 chapter 26 refers solely to indigenous people.

Thanks to a network of indigenous and supportive NGOs, these brief mentions of traditional knowledge in the Convention were expanded into a much larger issue, gaining increased attention for traditional knowledge and its protection. Every other year since 1996, when the parties have met to discuss the implications of the Convention, traditional knowledge has been on the agenda. In 1997 a workshop on traditional knowledge was held in Madrid, and another followed in Seville a few years later. By 1998, the fourth convention of the parties to the CDB created an ad hoc, open-ended intersessional working group to look into traditional knowledge. Thus the secretariat of the Convention now has a permanent group of experts in charge of examining and unpacking Article 8j that meets roughly every other year. Another ad hoc open-ended intersessional working group on benefit sharing was created two years later. These two interrelated topics have gained such prominence that in early 2006 a huge preparatory meeting to the Eighth Convention of the Parties to the CDB was organized in Granada with a significant indigenous presence.

In step with the CBD, several other United Nations institutions such as the Food and Agriculture Organization (FAO), the United Nations Conference on Trade and Development (UNCTAD), UNESCO, the World Health Organization (WHO), and of course WIPO (the World Intellectual Property Organization) actively took up the issue of traditional knowledge rights, and there has been a flurry of activity since 1998.

As far back as 1982, WIPO and UNESCO had actually produced the first international instrument to address traditional knowledge, if only tentatively—the Model Provisions for National Laws on the Protection of Expressions of Folklore Against Illicit Exploitation. In 1998-1999, WIPO sent out fact-finding missions all over the world, and convened two round tables on Intellectual Property and Traditional Knowledge. In 2000, it established a special body for examining those topics—the Intergovernmental Committee on Intellectual Property and Genetic Resources, Traditional Knowledge and Folklore.

FAO revised its Undertaking on Plant Genetic Resources for Foods and Agriculture to harmonize it with the CBD, and came up in 2001 with the International Treaty on Plant Genetic Resources for Food and Agriculture. In its preamble (paragraph 7), the Treaty reads:

> The Contracting Parties recognize the enormous contribution that the local and indigenous communities and farmers of all regions of the world, particularly those in the centers of origin and crop diversity, have made and will continue to make for the development of plant genetic resources which constitute the basis of food and agriculture production throughout the world.

I should also mention among UN bodies UNCTAD, the UN conference on trade and development, and WHO, the World Health Organization. The former convened an Expert Meeting on Systems and National Experiences for Protecting Traditional Knowledge, Innovations and Practices in 2000, just as the latter began looking into benefit-sharing for the commercial use of traditional medicine.

Outside the United Nations sphere, multilateral banks started paying at least lip service to traditional knowledge rights. By 2001, there was a position of "Chief Knowledge Officer" for Africa at the World Bank. Mr. Gorjestani, the incumbent, would quote James D. Wolfensohn, then president of the Bank: "Indigenous Knowledge is an integral part of the culture and history of a local community. We need to learn from local communities to enrich the development process."

The World Trade Organization (WTO) itself was forced to abandon its attempts to stay aloof of the debates over local and indigenous knowledge. In the background lie significant conflicts. The US, who never ratified CBD, is very much a member of the WTO. While CBD is a UN instrument and as such has no means of enforcement, the WTO has heavy sanctions in store for non-complying members. The WTO is particularly concerned with issues of intellectual property rights: to be eligible to join the WTO, countries are required to commit to Trade-Related Intellectual Property agreements (TRIPs) set up in 1994. WTO provisions are not currently compatible with CBD, and the issue of precedence has become a standing argument. While claming to have no obligations to CBD, the WTO feels compelled to address it. Since the end of 1998, according to official documents, "the issue of protection of genetic resources, traditional knowledge and folklore, including those of indigenous peoples, has been under discussion in the TRIPS Council."

Until some time around the nineties, certain UN bodies, particularly the Food and Agriculture Organization (FAO), defended the public domain to a large extent. But the nineties were the decade of the Uruguay Round and TRIPs. As mentioned above, to become members of the World Trade Organization countries had to align their national laws with TRIPs, meaning that they had to adopt strong protections for international Intellectual Property modeled on the US system. As much as the UN and the WTO were at odds on some fronts, there is no doubt that UN bodies aligned themselves with the WTO on intellectual rights, and in that event "property" won the day (and the decade) over the public domain. So much so that the expression "Intellectual Property Rights" (IPR), has become a household fixture. From this point on there could be no intellectual rights that were not also property.

International Indigenous Declarations

Having followed the emergence since the 1970s of a pan-indigenous organization in Brazil, a country that has more than 220 ethnic groups dispersed over a very large territory, I can testify to the difficulties faced by the peoples in such an undertaking, particularly as regards representation, legitimacy and operationality. At the world level, those difficulties grow exponentially. Indigenous movements, with few exceptions, have lacked support from their own national governments, and have therefore relied on the UN and NGOs to advance both their organization and their claims. It was the UN that, starting in 1994, launched the two subsequent Decades of Indigenous Peoples, the Working Group on Indigenous Populations, and, since 2002, the Permanent Forum on Indigenous Peoples functioning as an advisory body to UN Economic and Social Council (ECOSOC). It was also the UN that was eventually able to bring about the adoption of the

Declaration of the Rights of Indigenous People in September 2007.

Thus it was through the UN that international indigenous coalitions and organizations emerged as significant political actors. But over time, as in Brazil in the 1980s and 1990s, indigenous organizations would become independent interlocutors. In retrospect one can see that, in a significant sense, NGOs, the UN, and international indigenous organizations were instrumental in each other's growth and maturity. They have developed together, heavily influencing each other's agendas.

A number of statements, resolutions, recommendations and declarations of regional and international scope were made by Indigenous Organizations on the issue of cultural and intellectual rights. Up until the end of the 1980s, cultural rights over artifacts, designs, archaeological remains, and material culture in general were included in their own declarations at a time when UN bodies such as UNESCO and WIPO were concerned with the protection of folklore. Although such cultural rights could well have been framed as intellectual rights (such as copyrights over traditional designs), the emergence of a claim to intellectual rights can be directly linked to the issue of traditional knowledge (TK), in respect to both genetic resources and sustainable "management" of ecological systems—so-called traditional ecological knowledge (TEK).

An interesting reversal also took shape that clearly mirrors the shift from a post-WWII universalist position that emphasized non-discrimination and political participation, as represented in the 1948 Declaration of Human Rights, to a minority rights emphasis in the later part of the twentieth century.

Thus, in 1984, the World Council of Indigenous Peoples ratified a Declaration of principles claiming that "the culture of Indigenous Peoples is part of mankind's cultural patrimony." Yet in 1992, less than ten years later, the rather different Charter of the Indigenous and Tribal peoples of the Tropical Forests (IAIP Charter) was issued in Penang, Malaysia. This charter claimed intellectual property rights over traditional technologies. In June of the same year, an Indigenous Peoples' Earth Charter was approved at the pan-indigenous parallel event to the World Summit in Rio de Janeiro, in which cultural rights appeared side by side with intellectual property rights.

Traditional Knowledge Regimes as Figments of Different Imaginations

One can sense in all of these documents—whether they are UN and WTO documents, national legislations, or pan-indigenous declarations—the extent of the influence of prevailing metropolitan ideas on the notion of indigenous rights. That influence works in two seemingly contradictory ways. On one hand, indigenous movements couch claims in terms of a language of rights that is likely to be recognizable and therefore successful in the international arena. James Clifford, in his famous piece on the Mashpee trial, demonstrated how a historical account is more likely to be convincing to a jury than a discussion of anthropological concepts on ethnic identity. One doesn't carry the day by disputing received wisdom. That is likely to be what Marilyn Strathern meant when she wrote (*a propos* feminist scholarship) that radical politics are conceptually conservative. So are indigenous declarations.

And yet they come up with issues that assert the specificity and difference of their knowledge. Ironically, this is the second way that ongoing metropolitan concepts prevail. These concepts assume a single regime can encompass myriad different historical and social traditional knowledge regimes. But more specifically, one can see metropolitan imagination at work in the way traditional people are led to represent their knowledge and the rights that might be attached to it. Strathern again says it best: "a culture dominated by ideas about property ownership can only imagine the absence of such ideas in specific ways."

It is relatively easy to detect how different sectors imagine indigenous knowledge. Simply put, indigenous knowledge is conceptualized as the negative of mainstream prevailing ideas. As such, indigenous people seem inextricably destined to impersonate the obverse of capitalism's possessive individualist assumptions. They have to carry the white man's imaginative burden in order to be heard, but living in an intellectual property world provides little chance of extracting their own imagination from it. Concepts don't really change; imagination is restricted to reversal of choices or inversion of agents.

In this, we are no different from others. A long time ago, in the first article I wrote, I showed that a messianic movement among the Ramkokekra-Canela of Maranhão, Brazil, structurally inverted the myth of the emergence of the white man and his power. A reversal of fortunes was the expected outcome of the reversal of myth, with Indians living in towns and neo-Brazilians living in the forest and hunting with bows and arrows.

The script remained the same, but had been inverted. There are no new concepts, only new choices and new protagonists.

When dealing with traditional knowledge concepts and regimes, imagination does not stray very far from home. The mainstream conceptualization of traditional knowledge reasons as if the obverse of the individual were everywhere the collective (*qua* a corporate individual). In contrast to our individual authorship, their knowledge and culture in general must surely be collectively authored. Instead of invention springing from the genius of the individual, their cultural inventions are the outcome of a collective but no less endogenous genius.

Starting with Montaigne's political philosophy, New World indigenous people have been credited with embodying a critique of capitalist accumulation and of property. In this avatar, indigenous people are deemed to have no sense of intellectual property and to share in freely circulating knowledge and information. They are held up as an antidote to the rest of the world and its devouring greed. They are expected to hold hands with Robert Crumb and protest the extension of eternal copyrights to Mickey Mouse. In short, they should be at the forefront of anti-IPR movements.

According to such (un)imaginative constructs, indigenous people are offered but one of two choices: collective intellectual property rights or a commons regime. Both choices force indigenous regimes onto procrustean beds. It is small wonder that, given those restricted alternatives, they tend to pragmatically favor the mainstream choice and argue for collective intellectual property rights, thus disappointing the hopes of anti-IPR sectors that traditionally were their supporters.

What if there were other possible forms of rights between people concerning things (the very definition of property according to MacPherson) besides the ones we have built in the last three centuries? What if there is no boolean logic to be expected here, not just a yes or no possibility?

Such characterizations of intellectual property constrain in interesting ways how indigenous people can make their claims, even as they also erase the differences between regimes. There are many more knowledge and cultural regimes than our feeble metropolitan imagination can conceive of. If only one took ethnography seriously, a whole catalog of alternative ways could be assembled.

But if they want to carry the day, indigenous people have to conform to expectations, not contest them. They have to make do with knowledge and culture as other people understand them and come to terms with the contradictions they might entail.

National Legislations

In contrast with the proliferation of instruments and international studies, specific national legislation on access to traditional knowledge and benefit-sharing in the broader context of access to genetic resources has been extremely slow in developing. Gene-rich countries are still cautiously gauging the effects of some of the boldest among them, such as the Philippines, Costa Rica and Peru—countries that have passed legislation on the topic. NGOs, both national and international, are taking different positions. And in Brazil, notwithstanding a very early legislation proposal in 1994 and a provisional decree in 2001, as of early 2009 there is still a lot of hesitation in the Government as to what the access law should look like.

At the regional and national levels, most action is "defensive." One protests against the appropriation and privatization of what is thought of as public domain or relevant to one's territorial identity. So India is able to invalidate a US patent on neem usage; COICA, a multinational Federation of Amazonian Indigenous Organizations, disputes a US patent on the hallucinogenic brew known as *ayahuasca* or *yagé*; the Brazilian government successfully challenges a Japanese trademark of "cupuaçu," a well-known Amazonian fruit.

Traditional Knowledge and Nationalism

This state of affairs, of course, has all kinds of effects. A quite significant one is the realignment of indigenous societies with Latin-American nationalisms. Whatever the reality of State's policies towards indigenous people might have been, an important dimension of their existence has consistently been their ideological position in the nationalist imagination. It is striking how reality and ideology comfortably followed totally independent paths. If we just stick to their ideological dimension, indigenous peoples' role in the Brazilian self-image greatly varies according to the historical period and whether the Indians one is talking about are alive or extinct. Extinct Indians, not surprisingly, have regularly been promoted since the Independence of Brazil in 1822 as foundational contributors to national identity.

Their past allegiance or at least their trade links to Portuguese in opposition to Dutch and other colonial powers were brought up in border disputes with Venezuela and British Guiana in the early twentieth-century—a move that enlisted them as part of and agents in Brazilian territorial claims to sovereignty. Live indigenous people were another matter. Starting in the mid 1970s, with mineral wealth being spotted all over the Amazonian region, indigenous people who lived on top of many of those resources were the target of a press campaign that deemed them unreliable in their loyalties to national states.

The joined issues of biodiversity and traditional knowledge counteract that general anti-Indian trend. This time a different nationalist wave enrolls them as allies against biological piracy, to the point that in 2004 an anti-piracy "vigilant indigenous villages" project was approved and is being put into place. The particularly sensitive issue of blood samples from Brazilian indigenous societies being held in foreign institutions and made available or sold to researchers has raised public indignation. While Yanomami complain about their relatives' blood being stored instead of properly destroyed at death, national outcry transforms Yanomami's culturally-specific claim into a protest of Brazilian indigenous blood and DNA being stored in scientific facilities outside Brazil. In short, indigenous knowledge and indigenous blood have been made part of Brazil's national heritage.

Being part of a national heritage is a double-edged sword: while it enhances indigenous symbolic status, it also turns indigenous people into "our Indians," a formula that encapsulates the inherent ambiguity of indigenous status.

Extreme Diffidence and the Rise
of Esoteric Knowledge

While the "indigenous" has recovered some nationalist currency, inside Brazil the story is much more complicated. One of the major breakthroughs of the Convention for Biological Diversity was the recognition of every country's sovereignty over its genetic resources. The easier way out for the state is clearly to translate sovereignty into property, a move that is in no way evident and that has stirred some controversy. As indigenous people and NGOs have argued, if genetic resources and biodiversity are still present in indigenous territories, this is due to indigenous custodianship. It follows that indigenous and traditional people in general should not suffer the expropriation of what they have allowed to subsist, and that biodiversity in indigenous land cannot be dissociated from what is called traditional ecological knowledge. The remarkable contrast in deforestation rates between indigenous territories and their surrounding highly deforested areas is taken as evidence of this. What could be called indigenous "cultivation of the forest" has been particularly well documented among the Tupian-speaking Urubu-Kaapor, but is likely to be much more widespread. According to ethnobiologist Bill Balee, who studied the ecological practices of the Kaapor and other indigenous groups, what appears as pristine forest is to a large extent indigenously managed forest. The argument of indigenous production of biological diversity is particularly compelling when applied to agrobiodiversity (biological diversity in domesticated crop varieties). It is well known that hyper selection of varities is dangerous, since a variety can be decimated entirely by a single pest. The story of the Irish potato famine from 1845 to 1849, where potatoes were of a single variety and were all wiped out by blight, is a paradigmatic example. Germplasm banks were established to conserve a wealth of varieties, but being situated out of the source area of the cultivars they cannot engender varieties resistant to new diseases. This is where so-called *in situ* conservation, in which plants co-evolve with their environment, becomes crucial. That task has been taken over for centuries by small agriculturalists, mostly indigenous, who take pride in the diversity of their gardens. Traditional people have conserved and actually enhanced agricultural diversity in the regions where crops originated, as bear witness the hundreds of potato varieties in Peru, manioc in the upper Rio Negro, and rice in India.

The Convention for Biological Diversity does not simply bestow sovereignty over genetic resources on States. It simultaneously recognizes indigenous and local communities' rights to control their knowledge and to share in the benefits. With such provisions megadiverse states, of which Brazil is one, are caught in the crossfire. On one hand, such States struggle in international fora over issues related to benefit-sharing when enforcement mechanisms meet with strong resistance from the major industrialized countries and their allies. Internally, however, these same countries have to come to terms with traditional peoples' claims over their knowledge and genetic resources that bear a disturbing similarity to the national states' own claims. Furthermore, the CBD is a UN instrument, and indigenous people have increasingly relied on UN fora to voice their concerns and claims independently of—and indeed short-circuiting—governmental representation.

As such they are a source of potential embarrassment to these governments. A paradigmatic example is the issue of mandatory disclosure of origin in patent applications, a provision that would allow a check of the legality of access to genetic resources in the first place, and that would therefore hasten benefit-sharing. The claim that mandatory disclosure should be enforced internationally is advanced by megadiverse countries both in the context of the CBD and at the WTO forum. Internally, however, while disclosure of origin has been made mandatory inside Brazil, the Brazilian Patent Office has become notorious for dragging its feet in implementing the rule.

Given the long standing internal colonialist policies vis-à-vis indigenous peoples, recognizing their rights over genetic resources and traditional knowledge is not an easy about face for most megadiverse countries. Who should grant access to genetic resources in traditional peoples' lands, and under what conditions? In Brazil, while the Ministry for the Environment has been upholding traditional peoples' claims, some other Ministries have opposed them. Most prominently, Brazilian biologists backed by the Ministry for Science and Technology have fought for unencumbered (or at least simplified) access to Brazilian genetic resources. They resent being included in the same generalized bio-paranoia with which the indigenous people greet their foreign biologist colleagues.

The enrollment of indigenous people in a vigilant militia against foreign bio-piracy has had some other unintended consequences. It has transformed traditional knowledge into strategic quasi-secrets of state, thus generating extreme diffidence in relation to any kind of researcher, Brazilian or otherwise. At the same time, it has elicited quasi-eschatological hopes and hence disappointments over benefit expectations. And as Alcida Ramos and Beth Conklin have noted, it has made what was formerly perfectly common-place knowledge and practice into something esoteric. I will discuss a telling example of this trend when developing the frog story. Almost any kind of knowledge is now imputed to be the possession of "our shamans," or rather "our *pajés*," an expression I discuss below in the context of the Krahó affair. Significantly for this discussion, indigenous meetings on traditional knowledge are represented as shamanic meetings, and extreme confidentiality is enjoined on participants. It might not be a simple coincidence that shamanic vocations, whatever their hardships and their cost, are on the rise among young political leaders in the Amazon.

In most camps, extreme suspicion is the rule. The multinational pharmaceutical industry tries to distance itself as much as possible from any potential conflict by claiming that high-throughput screening effectiveness is such that it renders irrelevant any clue that traditional knowledge could possibly provide. Or else by advocating a turn to exclusively synthetic molecules created at random, they would make nature itself irrelevant.

What other effects are there of the intense international and national mobilization around traditional knowledge? As I cannot go into every dimension of these effects, I will privilege some by looking at the pragmatic material they present.

Contracts, Associations, Projects

I begin with the issue of representation. Access to traditional knowledge hinges on so-called "informed consent" which, in the case of bio-prospection, includes provisions for the sharing of benefits. Without going further into the interesting aspects of the process of reaching "informed consent," one thing is clear: the issue of who actually is supposed to give that consent comes up immediately. This raises two major problems: What kind of representation regime is being established? What can be construed as legitimate representation, and how does it relate to other authority structures?

Let us start with the latter.

Contracts and agreements produce in fact what they implicitly assume; they create their own conditions of possibility. I have already mentioned the redefinition of the relations between people and knowledge that they introduce. Here I will look at the issue of who are the "legal representatives" entitled to sign contracts and bestow "informed consent." Having served in a US University Committee which looked at informed consent, as well as having devised a whole procedure for informed consent in the "field," I have a strong sense of the multiple translations and legal fictions necessary to the endeavor.

Following the logic that Mauss and, later, Lévi-Strauss have described, contracts, as forms of (legal) exchange create (legal) subjects. Although indigenous forms of representation have been recognized as having jural legitimacy in the 1988 Constitution (art. 232), and indigenous persons are acceptable legal subjects under Brazilian law, nevertheless, civil society associations with approved and explicit by-laws have been promoted as the most convenient parties to "projects" involving contracts, banks, government, and NGOs. Hence indigenous peoples are adhering to new associative forms and local indigenous associations, with elected presidents and directors, have been popping up everywhere. They follow a legal format that allows them to claim representivity, but the problem, of course, is how to adjust legality to legitimacy. At times these associations purport to represent only a sector of the people, such as the indigenous schoolteachers who have been increasingly influential in indigenous politics. When it comes to associations which are deemed to represent the people as a whole, influential indigenous factions or families are quick to seize their presidencies and directorships through some (preferably literate) man genealogically or at least politically affiliated with them. In those cases, there is a convenient degree of convergence between village chiefs and association presidents. Associations, however, tend to represent more than one village. The problem with most lowland indigenous societies is that each village is an autonomous political unit, and intra-village factionalism or political dissent translates into the creation of a new village. Associations are not supposed to follow the same fissionable logic, and soon a stark contradiction can develop between the authorities the indigenous people used to consider legitimate and the legal representatives in associations.

Village autonomy being the norm, the emergence of something like an "ethnic representation" or group of representatives in the form of association leaders is necessarily fraught with conflict. Links between political institutions that stress village autonomy and associations that purport to represent the ethnic group as a whole—and that are a source of economic and political leverage—are not automatically given; and while they can be painstakingly constructed and validated, they can as easily be undone. Rival associations may emerge, and accusations launched: as was the case in Peru with the Aguaruna contract with Searle *cum* the Missouri Botanical Garden; and also with the team led by Brent and Elois Berlin to work on Maya ethnomedicine in Guatemala.

The Krahó Imbroglio: Legitimacy, Mirroring, Collectivities and Pragmatic Understanding

A telling example could be taken from the Krahó, an indigenous group in the state of Tocantins, Brazil, and its dispute with a Medical School from São Paulo. (Given that I wrote my doctoral dissertation on the Krahó in what now seems like the late Jurassic era, my data here mostly relies on Tiago Avila's insightful account in his 2004 doctoral thesis.) The dispute originated in a bio-prospecting project. The Medical School had sponsored research on plants ritually used by the Krahó with effects on the central nervous system. As a second step, the School now wanted to do research on Krahó therapeutic plants in general. From the start it had signed an agreement with an association that only encompassed some Krahó villages. Not surprisingly, another Krahó association protested and questioned the former association's representativeness. After a long dispute, a provisional understanding was reached on March 26, 2003, and a document drafted. Significantly, it was signed by the presidents of four Krahó associations *as well as* by the headmen of eighteen different Krahó villages. Representatives of the "Ministério Público" (a collective federal ombudsman of sorts that has the Constitutional duty of legal assistance to indigenous people) formally signed as witnesses to the decision, and representatives of the National Foundation for Indian Affairs (FUNAI) signed along with the Indians. What I am drawing attention to here is the apparent redundancy of the Krahó signatures. The legitimacy of the four associations' presidents had to be backed by the village headmen who co-signed the document, as if representation through associations needed the reassurance and the explicit mandate of "customary" political authority.

What's more, we will see in a moment that the story was further complicated by the fact that present-day Krahó claim to be the juxtaposition of two different Gê-speaking groups who maintain some geographical distinctiveness.

Thus far, I have dealt with my second issue: what might be construed as a legal and legitimate form of representation? I insist on the word *construed* since the very idea of representation might have previously been totally absent among the Krahó. For what exactly is "customary" in the preceding account? As I have argued in previous work, there is a fallacy in the concept of customary law, in that it is made to mirror positive law in all its attributes.

There are several problems with "customary" as it is pragmatically used. It assumes that "custom" (another word for culture) is something given, merely in need of explication or codification. It further assumes that "the Krahó," "the Katukina," "the

Kaxinawa," or any other such ethnic units are unproblematic entities of the same kind as, say, a country. This
is relatively simple to understand, but what if our own
constructs of society, representation, authority and their
like have (or had) no equivalents whatsoever among
these people? The two seemingly opposed moves of
subordinating indigenous nations and empowering
them are both predicated on the existence of such
things as nations and local authorities—that is, specific
social entities and subjects with attributes of both rule
and legitimacy. From the very beginning of European
penetration in the sixteenth century, Francisco de
Vitoria spoke of indigenous "princes" and of their
dominion over territories, as if the existence of such
entities were natural. The whole procedure of the
Requerimiento, in which "indigenous nations" were
assembled for Christian evangelization, is predicated on
the existence of indigenous authorities with attributes
comparable to Spanish kings. In 1755 the Marquis of
Pombal, Portugal's prime minister, in a prefiguration of
British Indirect Rule, ordered that indigenous leaders
be recognized as such. This move amounted to an interesting exercise in political imagination, as Amazonian
principals were granted insignia and supposed realms of
authority irrespective of whether or not such authority
had previously existed—even as in practice, these
"native authorities" were given little more than a deco-
rative role.

The current archaeological emphasis on the
existence of chiefdoms along the Amazon—that is, of
centralized structures of power—seems to undermine
my argument. It has been argued that inter-fluvial
indigenous populations could well be the survivors of
more centralized riverine polities, continuing to exist as

non-centralized orders. No doubt powerful principals were met and described in the traveler's literature, and some were actively entangled or enrolled in colonial politics. Still, some defining attributes of authority were felt to be missing since every single witness in the sixteenth-century reported or repeated that Brazilian Indians lacked faith, law and king.

Pierre Clastres famously used this topos to argue for indigenous "societies against the State"—that is, actively opposed to state forms rather than simply stateless societies. Although I would not endorse that argument to its full extent, and while the formerly unproblematic concept of "society" might presently deserve scrutiny, Clastres touched on something important. People might have been more profoundly different in their institutions than we are able to realize, enclosed as we are in a political ontology that started in the seventeenth century.

What are the consequences of this chasm between their institutions and ours? The discussion above would seem to lead one to a claim of unbridgeable differences. Not so. Political imagination has always been perfectly able to build those bridges. No doubt, terms and concepts are imposed by the powers that be; no doubt, authorities are invented where they had not existed. And yet, as Mauro Almeida argues, following Newton Da Costa, a pragmatic understanding emerges out of seemingly irreconcilable ontological differences.

As a matter of fact, the authority to represent an indigenous group is manufactured in the very process of discussing it and entering into contracts in its behalf. Does that mean it is illegitimate or "inauthentic," a vexed concept that has brought nothing but trouble to our world? If we are to follow Latour and his reading of Gabriel Tarde, making collectivities emerge in context rather than finding them "ready made" is properly universal. Political speech—and other political acts, I would add—are what constitute societies, groups, collectivities.

In 1944, four years after ranchers attacked two Kraho villages killing more than 20 Indians, a territory of 3,200 km^2 was officially recognized as Krahó land. By most accounts, the Krahó were formed through the historical fusion of two different Gê-speaking groups, with the addition of a number of survivors from other Eastern Timbira ethnic communities. A few foreign individuals from linguistically related groups, mostly Apinayé, but also neo-Brazilians from neighboring small towns have trickled in as well, usually by marrying Krahó women. As Krahó, like every other Gê-speaking group, are uxorilocal, in-marrying men can claim residence with relative ease. While one particularly mixed village stands apart from all the others, there is otherwise a clear-cut political distinctiveness between two sub-groups, respectively occupying the South and the Northwest (plus a Northern extension) of the territory, who have respectively thrown in their lot with either an NGO or a charismatic neo-Brazilian official agent. Whether these two factions' claim to different origins is the source or the result of that political split might be difficult to ascertain. But there is no doubt that claims of difference in origin are reinforced—if they do not initially emerge—in specific political conjunctures. While Krahó villages split, or less often coalesce, according to lines of fission and fusion that are largely structural, a new principle of organization has been put in place by the politics of "projects." As Bruce

Albert has shown, "projects" from foundations or from the government have become a major organizing principle of contemporary indigenous politics and social movements in general. In local parlance, one "hunts" projects and in such "hunting" parties anthropologists are at once recruited. The expression "making a project," *fazer um projeto*, has come to mean in Amazonian social movements' vernacular something very close to receiving a grant, or a gift. Mauro Almeida and I were once approached by a rubber-tapper who asked us to "write a project" for his purchase of a karaoke device. As there was no electricity in the forest, he would store it, carefully wrapped, alongside his other lovingly possessed appliances. While in local parlance the focus is on the economic nature of projects, I suggest they should be understood as any combination of cultural, political and economic endeavors that involve or rely on external agents as well as the indigenous population. Land demarcation, recovery of cultural items from a museum, participation in a pan-Brazilian indigenous political organization, and subsidized economic ventures are all examples of such projects—endeavors always at once political, cultural and economic. The point I wish to make is that successful projects entail a kind of associational mode that is supposed, and in actual fact is required, to transcend the local politics of inter-village and factional disputes in everyday life. Not surprisingly, then, associations flourish in tandem with the coming-into-being and phasing-out of projects.

Krahó associations were no exception. The first was Mãkrare, which started in 1986 at about the time an NGO-sponsored regional initiative for the defense of Indian land unfolded, and culminated in the 1990 demarcation of Krahó land. Another association, Kapey, was founded in 1993 and had a direct connection to research on traditional cultivars and seeds in partnership with a major governmental agricultural research institute called Embrapa. Still another, Vyti-Cati, emerged in 1994 and had a role to play in a joint venture involving fourteen villages taken from five different Gê-speaking ethnic groups in connection to the production of fruit pulp. While this association was inter-ethnic rather than strictly Krahó, it did not encompass every Krahó village.

The Mãkrare association's claim to represent all Krahó was unchallenged from its inception in 1986 until the early nineties, but the foundation of Kapey in 1993 signaled the erosion of its pan-Krahó legitimacy. As a spin-off of the original Mãkrare, Vyti-Cati had its predecessor's political base. Claims for separate ethnic origins of the Mãkrare and Kapey were therefore rekindled in the perception of the two associations as representing separate political and geographical spaces. In 1999, Vyti-Cati was the association that signed the first agreement with the São Paulo Medical School, permitting research on traditional medicinal plants, and in the process bringing about the episode we are now discussing.

At this point in our story a new social group emerged. On March 24, 2003, the first day of the meeting, Krahó "shamans" or *pajés* assembled and sat together in a circle. Encircling them in turn were the village leaders, the elders, and the association representatives. As all Gê-speaking groups seem to favor a spatial sociological idiom, this distribution on the ground was a significant index, in this context, of a new order of collectivity. In fact the idiom was enacted on two separate levels. First, the meeting was taking place in a *sui generis* innovative "village," a kind of United (Krahó) Nations, separate from any specific village. This was a circular set of houses around a central plaza, very much like any other Krahó settlement, or for that matter any other village of Gê speakers, at least ideally. The houses, however, were not uxorilocal units, as in real villages, but rather something approaching embassies of the different villages. The circular pattern was eloquent and widely understood. Equally understood was the second spatial enactment, namely the circle of *pajés* and the surrounding ring of elders and village leaders. Thus, the Krahó set out to explicitly translate and visually perform the novel representative regime they were constrained to enter into by circumstances not of their own making.

A note is in order here about nomenclature. The Krahó word for what is commonly called "shaman" in anthropological jargon would be *wayaká*. However there is also a common pan-Brazilian term for shaman, derived from the Tupi language spoken by the coastal indigenous groups in which the institution was first described in the sixteenth century. That term is *pajé*. Very much in the same way as "shaman" has become a common term in anthropological *lingua franca*, *pajé* has become a common term in Portuguese as well as in the indigenous social movements. It is therefore *pajé* that is used as a rallying term for referring to local experts in medical or esoteric knowledge. Needless to say, this covering term elides all kinds of meaningful distinctions within the broad *pajé* category of the kind that are relevant in almost every indigenous society. Indeed in many of these societies there is no vernacular term that would encompass all these different specialists.

Irrespective of categorical distinctions, if we just stick to the Krahó term *wayaká*, there had been no such thing as a collectivity of *wayaká* prior to these developments. According to ethnographies of the Krahó based on fieldwork conducted in the 1950s by Harald Schultz and then by Julio Cesar Melatti in the early 1960s, there were usually no more than one or two *wayaká* per village, and these practiced their craft independently of one another. Besides, their career prospects were often quite dismal. Because they were held responsible for deaths as well as cures and would charge heavily for their services, they usually ended up being accused of witchcraft. At this point they would either flee, be ostracized or be killed.

In any case there was no such thing as a college of *pajé*, and the formation of such an order of shamans was a true innovation. As *wayaká* perform their healing procedures using large quantities of tobacco, they were given a (possibly tongue in cheek) collective name that could be translated as "people of the tobacco smoke." One *wayaká* who was also a village headman and held to be the "representative" of the *pajé* collective was asked to persuade his colleagues to collaborate with the Krahó associations. The newly instituted college of pajés then proceeded to discuss specialists' hierarchy, patients' referrals, and other procedural matters. Foremost amongst these matters was the request for the Brazilian state to sponsor the practice of traditional medicine. The reasoning was transparent. If Krahó medicinal knowledge was deemed important to a medical school, then it should be treated in the same terms as western (public) medical practice. Facilities should be provided and *pajés* and staff should be paid by the state. The mere suggestion horrified the Medical

School and embarrassed the representative of the Health Ministry. The Medical School was ready to provide Western medical assistance to the Krahó, as they had done in the Xingu indigenous park for decades, but could hardly be seen to condone—let alone sponsor—indigenous medicine.

This episode points to the mirroring effects that are found in every single transaction, especially juridical or political transactions, involving indigenous people and the larger society. Consider that while Krahó *wayaká* or *pajé* have been well described in the ethnographic literature and could thus easily be understood as traditional, a college of *wayaká* with referral procedures is an institutional novelty stemming out of a particular situation or transaction, namely a claim to state-supported "traditional medicine." The institution explicitly mirrors the structure of bio-medicine as it demands recognition from it. Is it thus less authentic? If so, what are we to say of the spatial form in which it has been rendered? The college itself is expressively performed in strictly traditional Krahó spatial and linguistic practices, showing that Krahó cultural resources were mobilized for the endeavor. The issue of traditionality versus innovation becomes extraordinarily entangled. On what grounds is one to render judgment? The morality of the story, contrary to what one might think, is not to decide on its "authenticity." Rather it is that "authenticity" is undecidable, and that the question in this context makes no sense whatsoever.

The Frog Story

It is high time to tell the frog story. The hoopla started in April 2003 when a letter signed by Katukina indigenous people from the state of Acre reached the Brazilian Ministry for the Environment. The letter asserted that the use of an arboreal frog secretion, which had by then spread to every major town in Brazil, was derived from Katukina traditional knowledge and was being unduly appropriated by others. Minister Marina Silva, who was from the state of Acre and a rubber tapper's daughter, committed herself to making this case into a positive example—i.e., as one where traditional knowledge rights would be upheld. How to make this work and how to establish exemplary rules of use was quite a challenge, but the effort was a welcome departure from the purely defensive attitude that had prevailed on both sides. I was brought in at this juncture—although I pointed out from the start that the case entailed some of the most difficult issues of traditional knowledge, hence was not well suited to become a paradigmatic success story. I drew attention to the fact that knowledge and use of the frog secretion was shared by a large number of indigenous people in Brazil as well as in Peru, and that it had long been described in both the ethnographic and the biochemistry literature. Simply getting the different indigenous groups to agree on the sharing of possible benefits would be hard enough, not to mention that Peru and Brazil had different laws on the subject. As the Ministry for the Environment insisted on taking up this specific case, I started work with herpetologists, molecular biologists, medical researchers from a major hospital in São Paulo, and of course the indigenous people and civil servants involved. I also enrolled a former doctoral student of mine, Edilene Cofacci de Lima, who was on the faculty of the University of Paraná, and had worked on the Katukina for her dissertation.

There is not space here to delve into the interesting minutiae, so I will fast forward to some of the results. This frog is primarily *Phyllomedusa bicolor*—although some other Phyllomedusae species might be used in supplementary way. Found everywhere in the Amazonian basin, *Phyllomedusa bicolor* was first described as far back as 1772. Despite its wide distribution in the Amazon, only a few indigenous societies in the west and southwest seem to have used its powerful secretion in humans (and actually also in dogs). We could establish that the present or former use of this frog's skin secretion (and of some other related frogs') was attested for most Panoan-speaking peoples, with the exception of those living close to great rivers such as the Conibo and Shipibo in Peru. Katukina, Marubo, Mayoruna (Matses, in Peru), Yawanawa and Kashinawa peoples, to name a few, all used the substance in similar ways. The name that designated both the frog and by extension its secretion was some variation of *kampô*, *kambô*, or *kampu*, but I'll use the word *kampô* for short.

When stressed, *Phyllomedusa bicolor* exudes a secretion through most parts of its skin. Once the secretion is extracted, the animal is released. While the process of stressing it by heating looks quite unpleasant to these frogs, it is not uncommon to find them in a kind of semi-domesticated co-existence close to the village. The secretion can be used at once or else dried for later use. Rubbing the substance onto small skin burns allows it to reach the blood system. A number of quite unpleasant symptoms ensue, such as nausea, swelling, tachycardia, and diarrhea but all of these can actually be easily halted with a simple cold bath in the river. The purpose in most groups was mainly to cure hunters—as well as their dogs, who often had to endure a similar treatment—of bad hunting luck. The treatment was known to increase alertness as well as endurance to hunger and thirst. In addition, the secretion was used to cure a condition for which Indians sometimes used the Portuguese term for "laziness," but which covers a wide range of states including fatigue, fever and lack of enthusiasm for social intercourse. Success with women was also held to be result of taking *kampô*, but one could speculate whether that was actually a side-effect of being a successful hunter. Either way, it appeared that erotic success was a major factor for the regional popularity of *kampô*. "Getting a toad vaccine" or a "toad shot" from neighboring Katukina had been a long-standing, if infrequent, practice of people from the town of Cruzeiro do Sul, and of rubber tappers.

How did this practice come to be known in major towns in Brazil? According to research by Edilene Lima, it appears that it spread along well-established *ayahuasca*-based religious networks. *Ayahuasca*, as already mentioned, is a hallucinogenic beverage prepared by combining a vine (*Banisteriopsis caapi*) and the leaves from a bush (*Psychotria viridis*) into a brew that is widely known under a number of different names among indigenous groups throughout western Amazonia. Panoan-speaking groups in Acre regularly use the concoction, often under shamanic guidance. Shamans themselves use it for their own incorporeal voyages.

The use of *ayahuasca* spread to rubber tappers in Acre, who tended to use it in a semi-clandestine way since it was thought to be a rather uncivilized indigenous habit. The local name of the brew was *cipó*, the generic Portuguese word for vine, whereas *ayahuasca* is originally a Quechua word. The status of *ayahuasca* dramatically changed when it was integrated into a number of urban religions. The first such religion was *Santo Daime*, started in the early nineteen thirties by a former rubber tapper living in the outskirts of Rio Branco, the capital of Acre. Another urban religion is the *União do Vegetal*. As shown by Bia Labate, and by Sandra Goulart, *União do Vegetal* originated in 1961 likewise with a constituency of rubber tappers and in the outskirts of the capital city of a small Amazonian state, Rondônia; but as it took root in big cities in the late seventies, it captured a mostly middle class following, and went on to build a strongly hierarchical organization. *União do Vegetal* is known to use a scientistic language due to the growing presence and influence of medical doctors, psychiatrists and psychologists in its ranks.

The pan-Brazilian urban network set up by these religions, and specifically by *União do Vegetal* and by *Santo Daime*, accounts for the wide diffusion of *kampó*, the frog secretion, at the end of the twentieth century. While *União do Vegetal* was responsible for introducing *kampó* to major Brazilian cities, the religion eventually suspended its use for medical security reasons. By then, however, urban healers connected to the more loosely organized *Santo Daime* were widely spreading *kampó*. After a former rubber tapper who had lived among the Katukina started delivering *kampó* cures to urbanites in the 1990s, Katukina themselves were sought after for curing. As shown by Edilene Lima and Bia Labate, Katukina men were soon enrolled and paraded about by New Age healers, providing the latter with indigenous spiritual certificates of origin. In one case I witnessed in São Paulo, *kampô* was presented as a sort of medical panacea, able to find by itself the organ affected in the patient's body and to provide a cure.

By the end of 2007, *kampô* had virtually become a household word in Brazil. A *kampô* green condominium development project sprang up outside Rio de Janeiro, while the young heroes in a children's movie released for Christmas on that same year were depicted as seeking *kampô*, the ultimate Amazonian treasure.

The *kampô* issue raised a number of nationalist flags. When an NGO dedicated to hunting down bio-piracy listed some patents derived from *kampô*, the Ministry of Foreign Affairs was moved to file suit and make an exemplary case of it. Yet, there were a number of problematic issues. There seems to have been scientific research on the properties of that specific frog skin secretion independently of the ethnographic evidence on traditional knowledge. Although there are a number of ethnological publications going back to 1925 on indigenous use of *kampô*, it looks as if biochemists were unaware of them until they received explicit communication in 1990 or 1991 by two Americans. Furthermore, the Convention for Biological Diversity was only signed in 1992 and ratified by Brazil in 1994.

I took the trouble, with the help of Jenn Schaffler, my research assistant, of tracking down the stories of biochemical and ethnological research and getting evidence on what could be called their undeniable "first contact."

The Biochemist's Story

Vittorio Erspamer (1909-1999) was a prominent Italian medical pharmacologist who very early on became interested in amines naturally produced by animal organisms. Along with his histology professor in Pavia, Vialli, he identified enteramine in 1937, and subsequently set out to find naturally-produced amines, including enteramine. This substance was later independently isolated as serotonin. Shortly after WWII, while a professor at Bari University, he started working on mollusks and frogs, and was able to find enteramine in salivary glands of two octopus species (*Octopus vulgaris* and *Eledone moschata*) as well as in two other mollusks. He also found enteramine in the skin of *Discoglossus pictus*, a southern European frog originally introduced from North Africa, Malta and Sicily. This discovery was published in *Nature* as early as 1951. Encouraged by these results, Erspamer devoted his research to studying active compounds in amphibian skin and tissues of mollusks. This interest continued after his move to Parma's Institute of Pharmacology in 1956 and eventually to the University of Rome's Institute of Medical Pharmacology in 1967. Since 1948, Erspamer and his team have studied 500 different amphibians and 100 mollusks.

From 1949 to 1964, Erspamer was struck on at least two occasions by the effects of peptides he found in *Eledone moschata*'s salivary glands (1949) and then in a South American frog skin, *Physalaemus biligonigerus* (1962). The latter species is found in Central and Northern Argentina, Paraguay, Uruguay and Southern Brazil.

"At this point of our research in peptides," he reported, "serendipity went off the scene, and a systematic collection of amphibians, all over the world, was undertaken with the precise purpose of investigating the occurrence in their skin of peptides, and other active molecules."

This collection amassed the 500 different amphibian species. The most important contributor to the total was Dr. José M.Cei, a Professor of Biology at the University of Mendoza, Argentina, who collected frogs from Patagonia to Mexico, and sent 200 amphibian species to Erspamer's collection. Another 100 species from Australia and Papua New Guinea were sent by Dr. Robert Endean, from the University of Queensland, Australia. The remaining 200 species came from contributors in such countries as South Africa, the Philippines, and Malaysia, while some more common amphibians were purchased from Holland. Erspamer himself went on collecting field trips to the Great Barrier Reef in Australia, the Philippines and South Africa.

The great interest in these peptides is due to a singular fact. It became clear, starting around 1962, that frogs produce peptides in their skin secretions that are also present or at least have analogous counterparts in mammalian tissues, particularly from intestines and brains. This led to what Erspamer eventually called, in 1981, the brain-gut-skin triangle. An intriguing procedure developed involving, first, identifying frog peptides, analyzing their pharmacological properties, and then searching for comparable molecules in mammalian guts and brains. Given this very peculiar property, by 1983 more than 2000 papers had appeared on frog skin peptides.

Erspamer was both a pioneer and an enduring major player in his field. His project was fundamental science: rather than focusing on the most pharmacologically promising peptides, his interest was to explore the astounding variety of molecules that frog secretions exhibited. He isolated some 50 peptides from no less than 10 different peptide families, describing their structure and their functional activities. He published hundreds of scientific articles, was nominated more than once for the Nobel Prize, without patenting anything.

For nearly forty years, Erspamer's team in Rome collaborated with a Milanese lab, Farmitalia Carlo Erba Research Laboratories, whose researchers did most of the structural studies and syntheses of the molecules. Ada Anastasi and Montecucchi were the main peptide specialists at Farmitalia.

Sustained interest in Phyllomedusae began in 1968. Phyllomedusinae is a sub-family of New World tree frogs, the Hylidae. Among the six different genera within the Phyllomedusae sub-family is the genus Phyllomedusa, consisting of some twenty known species in 1968, a number that has since soared to forty-eight. Among other results, Anastasi, Erspamer and their team identified caerulein, a peptide from the secretion of an Australian frog *Hyla caerulea*. Caerulein had a wide range of pharmacological effects in mammals: among others, it lowered blood pressure, and it induced defecation by contracting gastro-intestinal tissues and augmenting secretions. It was similar to a duodenal mammalian hormone that unleashed a formidable motility and secretions of the intestine. Caerulein or analogous molecules also proved to be present in the skin of several frogs from South Africa and South America. But the studies of Phyllomedusae that began in 1968 indicated a somewhat more potent caerulein-like peptide (that received the name of Phyllocaerulin) in some species, while other species, such as *Ph. rohdei* (from Brazil) and *Ph. Hypochondrialis* (from Argentina), lacked that peptide but produced others. Ten years later, Monteccuchi and Erspamer published the structure of sauvagine, a peptide from the skin secretion of *Ph. Sauvagei*, a frog from Argentina and Chile, with anti-diuretic and lowering blood pressure activity in mammals. Erspamer primarily used *Ph. sauvagei* for his studies, in part because of the abundant supply. By 1981, Erspamer had identified six families of peptides in ten species of Phyllomedusae and the latest, dermorphins, were opioids many times more potent than morphine.

In the decade following the 1979 article on caerulin, a plethora of papers on the genus Phyllomedusae (at the time classified as Phyllomedusin family) were written by Erspamer and his colleagues. In 1985, Erspamer and his colleagues published what would become a widely cited article praising the unique and exceptional interest of the skin of the Phyllomedusa genus. They wrote:

> [T]heir cutaneous tissue appears to be an inexhaustible mine of these molecules (peptides). No other amphibian skin can compete with that of the Phyllomedusae, which has already yielded as many as 23 peptides belonging to at least seven peptide families.

The paper, originally a conference presentation but published in 1985, was suggestively titled *"Phyllomedusa*

Skin: a Huge Factory and Store-House of a Variety of Active Peptides." In the paper, Erspamer compared the quantity of four active peptides in the skin of eleven different frogs from the Phyllomedusin family, eight of which are from the genus Phyllomedusa. Although the peptides are similarly present in the different species, the quantities of these peptides are strikingly different. *Phyllomedusa bicolor* stands out among the eleven as the species with the highest concentration of the four peptides.

Then, around 1990, Peter Gorman, an American traveler and free lance journalist, writes to Erspamer describing his 1986 experience with what he calls *sapo* ["toad" in Spanish] among the Matses of the Rio Lobo, in Peru. He goes into details of the physiological and neurological effetcs of the substance.

The following is an extract from Gorman's account, published in 1993:

> I let Pablo burn my arm a second time. He scraped away the burned skin, then dabbed a little of the sapo onto the exposed areas. Instantly my body began to heat up. In seconds I was burning from the inside and regretted allowing him to give me a medicine I know nothing about. I began to sweat. My blood began to race. My heart pounded. I became acutely aware of every vein and artery in my body and could feel them opening to allow for the fantastic pulse of my blood. My stomach cramped and I vomited violently. I lost control of my bodily functions and began to urinate and defecate. I fell to the ground. Then, unexpectedly, I found myself growling and moving about on all fours. I felt as though animals were passing through me, trying to express themselves through my body. It was a fantastic feel-

ing but it passed quickly, and I could think of nothing but the rushing of my blood, a sensation so
intense that I thought my heart would burst. The
rushing got faster and faster. I was in agony. I gasped
for breath. Slowly, the pounding became steady and
rhythmic, and when it finally subsided altogether. I
was overcome with exhaustion, I slept where I was.
When I awoke a few hours later, I heard voices. But
as I came to my senses... I realized I was alone. I
looked around and saw that I had been washed off
and put into my hammock. I stood and walked to
the edge of the hut's unwalled platform floor and
realized that the conversation I was over hearing was
between two of Pablo's wives who were standing
nearly 20 yards away. I didn't understand their
dialect, of course, but I was surprised to even hear
them from that distance. I walked to the other side
of the platform and looked out into the jungle; its
noises, too, were clearer than usual.

And it wasn't just my hearing that had been
improved. My vision, my sense of smell, everything
about me felt larger than life, and my body felt
immensely strong.

Erspamer was clearly excited by Gorman's report of his
experiences; he carefully compared them to his laboratory results. He was thus able to find a biochemical
explanation for all the symptoms but one. It so happens
that the exception he makes is indeed a symptom that
never appears in descriptions other than Gorman's.

Indeed, Gorman published and commented on
a letter that Erspamer would have sent him by mid
1991, with his results:

Based on the concentrations and functions of the
peptides found in and extracted from the sapo sample

I sent, Erspamer was able to account for all of the physical symptoms I described as sapo intoxication. On the peripheral effects, Erspamer reported, "Caerulein and the equiactive phyllocaerulein display a potent action on the gastrointestinal smooth muscle and gastric and pancreatic secretions.... Side effects observed (in volunteer patients with post operative intestinal atony) were nausea, vomiting, facial flush, mild tachycardia (heart palpitations), changes in blood pressure, sweating, abdominal discomfort, and urge for defecation.

Phyllomedusin, a new peptide of the tachykinin family, strongly affects the salivary glands, tear ducts, intestines, and bowels: and contributed to the violent purging I experienced. Sauvagine causes a long-lasting fall in blood pressure, accompanied by severe tachycardia and stimulation of the adrenal cortex, which contributed to the satiety, heightened sensory perception, and increased stamina I described. Phyllokinin, a new peptide of the bradykinin family, is a potent blood-vessel dilator and accounted for the intense rushing in my blood during the initial phase of sapo intoxication.

"It may be reasonably concluded," Erspamer wrote, "that the intense peripheral cardiovascular and gastrointestinal symptoms observed in the early phase of sapo intoxication may be entirely ascribed to the known bioactive peptides occurring in large amounts in the frog material."

As to sapo's central effects, he wrote, "increase in physical strength, enhanced resistance to hunger and thirst, and more generally, increase in the capacity to face stress situations may be explained by the presence of caerulein and sauvagine in the drug. Caerulein in humans produces an analgesic effect... possibly related to release of beta-endorphins... in patients suffering from renal colic, rest pain due to

60

peripheral vascular insufficiency (limited circulation), and even cancer pain." [...]

The sauvagine extracted from sapo was given subcutaneously to rats and caused release of corticotropin (a hormone that triggers the release of substances from the adrenal gland) from the pituitary with consequent activation of the pituitary-adrenal axis. This axis is the chemical communication link between the pituitary and the adrenal glands, which controls our flight-or-fight mechanism. The effects on the pituitary-adrenal axis caused by the minimal doses given the laboratory rodents lasted several hours. Erspamer noted that the volume of sauvagine found in the large quantities of sapo I described the Matses using would potentially have a much longer lasting effect on humans and would explain why my feelings of strength and heightened sensory perception after sapo use lasted for several days.

But on the question of the "magical" effects I described in tapir trapping, Erspamer says that "no hallucinations, visions, or magic effects are produced by the known peptide components of sapo." He added that "the question remains unsolved" whether those effects specifically, the feeling that animals were passing through me and Pablo's description of animas projection were due to "the sniffing of other drugs having hallucinogenic effects, particularly nu-nu."

Those same results were published in Erspamer's and collaborator's 1993 article under the expressive title of "Pharmacological studies of Sapo from the frog *Phyllomedusa bicolor* skin—a drug used by the Peruvian Matses Indians in shamanistic hunting practices."

As mentioned above, what is particularly remarkable in Erspamer's article is that it provided a biochemical explanation for almost every symptom described by Gorman, with a notable exception: his account of something close to hallucination—a sensation of animals passing through his body—which Erspamer found impossible to attribute to the secretion itself. This exception is particularly telling, since there are no corroborating ethnographic reports of hallucinations due to the frog secretion, making Gorman's report idiosyncratic in that respect.

The Ethnographers' Story

The first undeniable record of the use of *kampô* by indigenous groups came from Constantin Tastevin, a French missionary of the *Congrégation du St Esprit*, an order that had monopolized missionization along the Juruá river since the late nineteenth century. Given the rubber boom during this period, the mission's field was highly promising in terms of collecting revenue, if less successful in collecting souls. Tastevin's writings can be roughly divided into two periods. Starting as a straightforward missionary from deep Brittany, he wrote edifying and patronizing anecdotes in major Catholic mission journals, along with more candid reports to the *Congregation*. Then at some point around the 1910s, Paul Rivet, the co-founder with Marcel Mauss and Lucien Lévy-Bruhl of the Paris Institute of Ethnology in 1925, became interested in Tastevin's Amazonian expertise, and suggested they co-write articles in linguistic and anthropological journals. This is when

Tastevin re-invented himself as an ethnographer and a human geographer, penning a series of important articles on the then little known upper Juruá region. His writings were of such importance that during World War II, as rubber once again became a strategic commodity for the US, every one of Tastevin's geographical articles was translated into English. Although never published, these translations were most likely for US intelligence use. Tastevin's second life as an ethnographer of Western Brazilian Amazon landed him in 1927 at the *Institut Catholique* in Paris where he held for a brief period the chair of ethnology.

In a paper published in 1925 in *La Géographie* describing the Muru River area in the Upper Jurua basin, Tastevin described the procedure and the effects of the frog secretion among the Kulina and reported its use among Kaxinawa and Kanamari peoples. Kaxinawa, he wrote, attribute the origin of *kampô*, and many other precious things both tangible and intangible, such as axes, *ayahuasca* (*honi*), snuff and even the night to Jaminawa, "People of the Night." Rather than an ethnonym proper, Jaminawa, as Barbara Kieffenheim has argued, appears to denote a generic position, that of provider of goods, with each Panoan-speaking group having its Jaminawa as their own supplier of axes. Still, this is an indication of a trait that we will discuss at some length, namely the indigenous propensity for attributing major cultural items and knowledge to other groups. As if by definition, one's own culture was the result of appropriation, a cultural predation of sorts.

The second unambiguous mention of the indigenous use of *kampô* came from the Tikuna, a linguistically isolated group on the upper Solimões, in the state of Amazonas. It could be the case that knowledge of the substance and of its use spread from inter-riverine panoan-speaking groups to their northern neighbors Kulina and Kanamari and from the latter to the Tikuna. At any rate, in 1955, a zoologist, Jose Candido de Melo Carvalho, published a report from his 1950 expedition indicating a similar use of a frog by the Tikuna, who called it *bacururu*. This publication was the first to provide the identification of the frog as *Phyllomedusa bicolor*.

The first mention of the use of frog skin secretion in English appears to be a 1962 article by anthropologist Robert Carneiro from the American Museum of Natural History, followed by another in 1970. Carneiro described the use of the secretion for hunting magic among the Panoan-speaking Amahuaca of Peru, and the description of the posology and effects coincided in every detail with previous ones. Carneiro was unable to identify the frog, but Amahuaca called it *kambó*, a name that is close enough to our *kampô*. Since Carneiro described it as a small frog, however, uncertainty remains as to whether it is the same as the rather large species *Phyllomedusa bicolor*.

Numerous other mentions of this practice and of the frog followed, particularly among Panoan-speaking inter-fluvial indigenous groups in Brazil, such as Matis (by Erikson), Matses (by Romanoff in 1984) and Marubo (by Montagner Melatti in 1985). The secretion is used in a strikingly different manner among Tukanoan-speaking Barasana of Colombia for obtaining yellow feathers from tame birds. This case, reported in 1973 by Stephen Hugh-Jones is exceptional as most cases reported follow the panoan pattern. While data on the use of *kampô* by a number of indigenous societies steadily grew, there is no evidence that biochemical researchers were aware of the ethnographic literature up until the 1980s.

Then two Americans entered the scene: Peter Gorman, the already-mentioned traveler, and a biological anthropologist from Berkeley, Katherine Milton. As we saw, Gorman claims to have first undergone *sapo* treatment among the Matses in 1986. Although he returned the following year, it was only around 1989 that he was given a stick with dried *sapo* substance, and was able to take photographs. He reported giving half that stick to the curator of herpetology at the American Museum of Natural History, Charles Myers, who passed it on to John Daly, a biochemist then working at the National Institute of Health. Daly was well versed in amphibian biochemistry, having studied tropical dart frogs (from genus Dendrobates) whose poison was traditionally used on arrow tips. Daly became the main author of a new crop of scientific articles. Then, Gorman obtained more dried secretion, and two live specimens from the Matses. One of the specimens died soon after getting to the US, and was sent to Daly. The other specimen, Gorman reports was sent to Vittorio Erspamer in Italy who extracted 126mg of skin secretion, and identified it as *Phyllomedusa bicolor*. According to Erspamer, the specimen was received in February 1991.

Meanwhile Katherine Milton, while studying ecology and indigenous diet in the Amazon under the sponsorship of the National Geographic Society, spent some time among the Mayoruna in Brazil. Although Gorman and Milton were respectively in Peru and Brazil, the locations of their fieldwork were only some 60kms from each other, and they were working with the same indigenous society, for Mayoruna is the Brazilian name for the Peruvian Matses. Matses' use of the frog secretion had been reported in Romanoff's 1984 Ph.D. dissertation, and it is likely that Milton was aware of that data. She did not report taking the substance, but described and photographically illustrated the entire preparation of the frog secretion in a 1994 publication, and took some 400mg of dried secretion to John Daly in the US.

By 1992, Daly and his collaborators (including Charles Myers and Katherine Milton) published the first biochemical article in which reference was made both to traditional indigenous use of *Phyllomedusa bicolor* and to ethnographic literature on Panoan-speaking groups. The article concerned the isolation of a peptide named adenoregulin. The following year, Erspamer and his collaborators published a comprehensive article that tallied the molecules identified in the secretion with the physiological effects reported by Gorman. Thus for the first time in his copious scientific production on Phyllomedusae, Erspamer mentioned and took accurate note of a number of ethnographic sources. In other words, Daly's 1992 paper and Erspamer's from 1993 provide the first irrefutable proofs of an awareness by the scientific literature of the existence of traditional indigenous knowledge on *Phyllomedusa bicolor*. The integration of biology and ethnography had begun.

Whatever the situation prior to that date, there is no doubt that by 1992, the year the Convention for Biological Diversity declared genetic resources to be under the sovereignty of states and traditional knowledge to be entitled to a fair share of benefits, biologists were fully apprised of the ethnographic data.

I shall not recount the flurry of activity and patents related to Phyllomedusa-derived molecules that followed in the nineties and the twenty-first century. Patents in general became ever more common during this period, with universities pressuring researchers to patent their inventions before publishing, and the TRIPs ensuring that more and more countries would be led to respect them.

To tie up the (provisional) end of this story, several attempts were made to construct this case as a model of collaboration between scientific and traditional knowledge. So far, all have failed. The industry was approached by the Ministry for the Environment and showed interest in signing contracts (and ensuring royalties) both with scientific institutions and indigenous people. The former objected and would acknowledge no input whatsoever from the indigenous people. Similar reasons account for the aborted second attempt, which proposed the establishment of a molecular biology lab jointly chaired by indigenous people, the university, and the Government of the state of Acre in order to undertake research on Phyllomedusae secretions.

Interestingly enough, the indigenous people turned to a more familiar solution. Rather than insisting on scientific precedence or input, the Katukina took the cultural turn once again. With money from the German government, and the support of the Brazilian Ministry of the Environment, they started a "House of Culture" in one of their villages where people could come for a "traditional *kampô* session."

"Culture" vs. Culture

I wrote above on the limited imagination that is at the basis of international and national provisions for indigenous knowledge. Ultimately, that imagination is predicated on a notion of "culture" of which knowledge is but one manifestation. In other words, the way Indigenous Intellectual Rights are conceived of relies on how culture is understood.

As is widely known, "culture" in its anthropological and by now juridical usage, comes from eighteenth century Germany, and was linked from its inception to the notion of some quality, some original spirit or flavor, that united people into nations while separating nations from each other. It was also inherently linked to the idea that such originality sprang from different peoples' distinctive views of the world—of which, moreover, they were the "authors." A sense of collective and endogenous authorship remains to this day. How well these and other assumptions or connotations are universally applicable is a matter of significant ethnographic attention.

Anthropologists such as James Leach, Marilyn Strathern, Deborah Gewertz, Simon Harrison and others have convincingly shown how unfit for Melanesia some of our own notions of culture and intellectual property are, and I will discuss below some illuminating examples taken from there as well as from the Amazon.

Though relying on such examples, however, I want at this point to discuss something else. Namely, how indigenous people reconcile—both in practice and intellectually—the limited understandings that they are deemed to perform with their own imagination. I look into both the pragmatic uses of "culture" and "knowledge" by indigenous people, and into the logic that can overcome contradictions between metropolitan and indigenous imaginations. How do people use cultural performance and the category of "culture" itself? How can people simultaneously hold different (if not opposed) expectations without there being a sense of contradiction?

Asking these kinds of questions returns us to classical anthropology. Such an inquiry was at the root of Evans-Pritchard's magnificent 1936 book on *Witchcraft, Oracles and Magic among the Azande*. Demonstrating the power of ethnography, he argued that contradictions were not perceived by the Azande because the practical social rules implicating beliefs maintained a strict separation of contexts, such that that no overt contradiction could ever surface. This may well also be the case in the very different situation we are dealing with. Positing, as most national legislations do, that customary rights should govern the internal allocation and distribution of benefits is a way of trying to separate internal from external contexts.

In a previous text, presented in 2002 in Barcelona under the title "Culture in Politics: intellectual rights of indigenous and local people," I argued that one should distinguish between contexts. Yet this was not just in order to pragmatically avoid the surfacing of contradictions, as in the Azande case; it was rather an argument about logic. I suggested that one should distinguish the internal logic of endemic contexts from the inter-ethnic logic that is paramount in other situations. A note of caution is in order: inter-ethnic logic is not equivalent to submitting to outside logic, nor to that of the most powerful. Instead it is a way of organizing a relationship to such other logics. For, as I have argued on many occasions since 1979, inter-ethnic situations do not lack structure. Rather, they cognitively and functionally self-organize.

Here is an example of inter-ethnic cultural articulation: in his *History* (Book 1. 82) Herodotus tells us of the two battles over the town of Thirea in which the Argives lost to the Lacedemonians. "Pursuant to these events," writes Herodotus,

> the Argives cut their hair short, whereas formerly they were compelled by law to wear it long, and they made a law with a curse attached to it, that from that time forth no man of the Argives should grow the hair long. The Lacedemonians, however, laid down for themselves the opposite law, to this, namely that although they had previously had short hair, from that time forward they should wear it long.

In this example, the point is not that the reversal of hairstyles among Argives and Lacedemonians really happened, but that it was considered plausible that people would change their customs for the sake of inter-ethnic oppositions.

This kind of process—the organization and enhancement of cultural differences—has attracted more attention in colonial and post-colonial studies. But inter-ethnic logic is not predicated on a colonial situation, nor to a power differential in general. As Sahlins has pointed out, Bateson's schismogenesis and Lévi-Strauss' *Race and History*, *The Myth of Asdiwal* and the four volumes of *Mythologiques*, already deal with the articulation between different groups of people, irrespective of their relative power. In a sense, the idea of inter-ethnic articulation follows seamlessly from Lévi-Strauss's theory of totemism and the organization of differences. In contrast to an endemic context in which logic operates on units or elements that are part of a social whole, in an inter-ethnic situation, it is societies as a whole themselves, ethnic groups, that are the units of the inter-ethnic structure. They are its constituent elements, and they derive meaning from it.

What this entails is that traits that have a significance derived from their position in an internal cultural scheme are functioning simultaneously as meaningful elements of inter-ethnic contrasts. They are part of two systems at once and there are consequences attached to this. In order to be more precise in the definition of "culture" that was only alluded to at the beginning of this pamphlet, I have suggested earlier we use the quotation marks—"culture"—for cultural units as elements in an inter-ethnic system.

"Culture" belongs to a meta-language: it is a reflexive notion that speaks about itself. Now the general problem is this: how can one operate simultaneously under the aegis of "culture" and culture, and what are the consequences of this predicament? What happens when "culture" contaminates and is contaminated by that of which it speaks, that is culture? What happens when "culture" is, so to speak, present in one's mind alongside that which it is supposed to describe? If those who are culture practitioners, those who produce culture while reproducing it, think of themselves under the two species, of which one is conceived of in theory (even as it is not in fact) as the totality of the other? What are the effects of reflexivity on these matters?

Before we get into this, let me spell out a simple working definition of culture without quotation marks. Lots of perfectly good trees have been felled for the sake of the unending squabbles on that matter, and I will not waste further branches describing them. I will even go further: in order to stay away from my discipline's controversies, I will adopt a literary scholar's definition that seems to sum up particularly well what has trickled down from anthropology to everyman's received wisdom. Here is what Lionel Trilling wrote in *Sincerity and Authenticity*:

> [the idea of culture in its chief present-day meaning], the idea, that is to say, of a unitary complex of interacting assumptions, modes of thought, habits, and styles, which are connected in secret as well as overt ways with the practical arrangements of a society and which, because they are not brought to consciousness, are unopposed in their influence over men's minds.

The comment on (un)consciousness could be disputed, but I shall let it pass here since it is incidental to my present argument.

The starting point of my previously mentioned 2002 paper was the following conundrum. Organizations with which I tend to align myself as a citizen recommend that traditional knowledge be put in the public domain, or more accurately in the *domaine public payant* (for historical reasons always in French). What this means is that traditional knowledge, deemed collective by definition, is made accessible to everyone (including everyone in the collectivity), but that its originators are entitled to payment if anything is derived from it of commercial value. Yet, as we shall see below, many traditional societies conceive of private rights over knowledge. I even suggested a somewhat paradoxical correlation: the less a society conceives of private rights over land, the more it seems to have developed rights over "intangible material," of which knowledge is a prime example. How then can one support a project that entails *domaine public payant* for traditional knowledge while at the same time knowing full well that this is often contradicted by customary right?

My conclusion was that such a contradiction could be solved if one notices that when considering customary rights, one is moving in the realm of cultures (with no quotation marks), whereas when considering alternative well-intentioned law proposals one is in the realm of "cultures."

It follows that two arguments can be simultaneously true.

Intellectual rights exist in several traditional societies: this pertains to culture. There is a political project which includes indigenous as well as non-indigenous organizations that envisages putting traditional knowledge into the public domain (*payant*): this pertains to "culture."

What might appear as a sleight of hand is in fact a consequence of the reflexivity I have mentioned.

Reflexivity and Its Effects
(With Thanks to Mauro Almeida)

We know, since Bertrand Russell, that reflexivity is the
mother of all paradoxes of "the liar" type. The Cretan
who says of himself "I lie," is both lying and not. For if
he is lying, he is saying the truth; and if he is not, then
he is lying. The paradox, as Bertrand Russell was the
first to remark, derives from the Cretan's dangerous
capacity to speak about his own speech. Every language
that is allowed to speak of itself is endowed with the
ability of rigorously establishing the simultaneous truth
and falsity of some propositions. This, of course, is the
case of ordinary language. But it is also, as Alfred Tarski
has established in the 1930s, the case of many other
sub-languages. What all such languages have in
common is that they authorize citation. Usage of
"quotation marks" is an example of that recourse. Any
language rich enough to allow for citations, and therefore endowed with self-reference, is conducive to paradoxes. One has the choice of either being unable to say
everything—and the language will be incomplete—or
of being allowed to say everything but being led in that
case to posit contradictory sentences. One has to opt,
and this is Gödel's theorem, either for completeness or
for coherence. Russell, of course, chooses coherence.
But only logicians and lawyers will prescribe coherence.
Common choice rather privileges completeness, and
that is why we, anthropologists who deal with common
sense, are more interested in complete languages. As
does almost everyone else, Native Brazilians included.

It is thus quite consciously and in line with a
classic convention about reflexivity that I chose to place

"culture" in quotation marks when referring to what is said of culture.

People are—more often than one tends to admit—aware of their "culture" or something resembling it, as much as living *in* culture. Examples are legion, and I will describe a few in a moment. Lévi-Strauss admits of this co-presence of "culture" and culture in his famous *Introduction* to the work of Marcel Mauss. Here he contrasts natives' exegesis, which is part of what it purportedly describes, to that of the anthropologist, which is deemed to be detached from it. Franz Boas' "coming to consciousness" of culture is certainly no novelty, nor is it just a contemporary or colonial phenomenon: self-awareness of *kerekere* as a Fijian custom, as Sahlins has shown, preceded British Rule rather than being derived from it. Thus, objectifying culture, contrary to the arguments of many anthropologists, did not start with colonialism. British anthropologist Simon Harrison, for one, in his 2000 paper on the objectification of culture in Melanesia, has reviewed the ever expanding anthropological literature on the multiple and old testimonies of the reification of culture throughout Melanesia, the pre-colonial period included.

If this is the case, then people tend to live simultaneously in both "culture" and culture. Analytically, however, these two spheres are not the same, as they rely on different principles of intelligibility. The internal logic of culture does not coincide with the inter-ethnic logic of "cultures."

One source of my interest in this point, besides my mathematical training, is a powerful side remark of Louis Dumont, which he modestly called idiosyncratic, but which is most revealing in this discussion. In his

"Introduction to Two Theories in Social Anthropology," Louis Dumont stressed that what things are depends on the set of things of which they are a part. Contrary to one's perception, things cannot be defined in themselves, but rather as elements of this or that system. By system we should understand an organized set, with its internal logic.

The issue, then, becomes how people come to terms with living in "culture" as well as in culture.

Not only are meta-cultural terms that speak about culture pervasive in Melanesia, according to Harrison, but cultural traits are constituted as objects or quasi-objects as they figure in all kinds of transactions: rights over rituals, songs, magical know-how, or spells can be offered or sold, received as gifts or bought. According to Margaret Mead's 1938 description of the Arapesh, mountain people would acquire their rituals from coastal people and after a while sell them to third parties in order to buy new ones. There were even societies specializing in cultural production for export, as Harrison nicely puts it. The Mewun of Vanuatu were producers of *kastom*, the pidgin word often translated as "tradition": they would provide their neighbors and hence (since this is Melanesia) their neighbors' neighbors with intangible goods such as dances, songs, and rituals. Cultural goods were thus construed as property —by which we understand a cultural bundle of rights— and jealously guarded. But they were not inalienable. Rights over cultural goods were subject to transactions that could take a range of different forms. For example, one could have what we would describe as outright sale of rights over ornamental motifs and designs, with the previous proprietors relinquishing any claim to use the same motifs in decorating their own houses. More often than not, a kind of "franchise" was put in place. One could alienate the right of performing a dance, for example, while retaining other proprietary rights over it. What seems to have mattered was less an exclusive right of performance than the exclusive right to authorize cultural borrowing or acquisition. Christian religions were also made part of this system—so much so that, according to Neumann, Methodist missionaries were killed in 1878 for extending their religion from old converts' to neophytes' villages before the necessary inter-village transactions dealing with claims over Christianity were concluded. Rights of cultural adoption could fit in the wide range of other goods that circulated in exchange networks involving marriage or commercial partnerships. The distinction between tangible and intangible items, that is the status of the items themselves, was secondary to the well-established primacy of exchange relations.

As in many other domains, Amazonian and Melanesian societies share some of these characteristics. Almost everywhere in the Amazon, customs, songs, ceremonies, knowledge and know-how have a foreign origin by definition. Fire has been taken from the jaguar or from the vulture. Ornaments and songs are received from spirits or conquered from enemies. As if there were a kind of generalized cultural fetishism, these societies seem to misrecognize what we would deem to be their own creations. This misrecognition could be linked to the prestige that attaches itself to exotic goods; however, the prestige of foreign customs and commodities in itself begs for explanation, and can be expressed in different modalities. In the Amazon, for instance, it rests on a concept of culture as loan, on the opening to the Other that Lévi-Strauss has stressed in

Histoire de Lynx. Rather than keeping strangers at bay, Amazonians display an appetite for the "Other" and her cultural trinkets that goes to cannibal extremities. This is strikingly different to the policy of the Chinese emperors who, as Sahlins pointed out, would store European presents—telescopes, carriages and other objects meant to impress them—in some kind of cabinet of curiosities. Useless in terms of identity, such objects would not be assimilated by the Emperor but instead were relegated to country palaces. Sixteenth-century France too had its *cabinets de curiosités*. The persistent vogue of exoticism in France can probably be dated from that century: one finds in the Louvre native Brazilian rattles mounted on gold bases during the reign of Henri II. The value attributed to the exotic in France, however, requires that it retains a foreign quality, by remaining part of a different system. Certainly, it can be a prop for class distinction, but always as an object from a different world—to assimilate it would destroy its value. It is likely that this social distance is what allowed for sociological comparison as practiced by Jean de Léry, and most of all Montaigne, as they mirrored and opposed the customs of their land to those of Brazil.

In the Amazon, by contrast, one does not keep a distance from the foreigner and the foreign: as Eduardo Viveiros de Castro has suggested, one incorporates them (and it is here that the cannibal metaphor is precisely not a metaphor). The same voracity prevails, as we just saw, for cultural traits. In such a universe, as Viveiros de Castro puts it so well, culture is always by definition acculturation.

A well-known example of such a regime of intangible goods is the one regulating personal names and associated privileges in Gê-speaking societies of Central Brazil. I will use an example from the Mebengokre-Kayapó as described in detail by Vanessa Lea, where a set of beautiful names is a limited good that should not be depreciated. Beautiful names confer all sorts of intangible riches called *nekrêt*, which consist of complex rights over things such as songs, ritual roles and ornaments. They also convey rights to certain parts of game meat for men, and for women to tame specific animals. The first beautiful names were acquired from fish, but shamans provide a steady flow of new names that they obtain in their nocturnal travels. These names and their associated prerogatives are property, and the holders of this kind of property are houses organized by matrilineal descent. If no one in the house is available in a given generation, however, names can be given in usufruct for life to people from other houses. The recipients will be responsible for bearing them, with the provision that they will pass the name on to proper members of the house of origin. The idea is that every name should be present in any given generation. But juridical figures that apply to names are not restricted to property and usufruct. Names can be borrowed, deposited in trust, stolen, and probably preyed upon or conquered.

A remark by Vanessa Lea allows me to return to my original point. Lea states that the Kayapó are not concerned with preserving names in general, but just those pertaining to their own specific maternal house. Should we conclude that culture has its own invisible hand, and is nothing but the general result of everyone's attachment to their own prerogatives? What I would rather note is that for the Kayapó, given the differentiated character of such attachment to the intangible wealth of one's own house, there is no sense of "culture" as a collective and shared patrimony.

There is a striking difference, as Simon Harrison has remarked, between culture understood in this fashion—subject to accumulation, borrowings and transactions—and what I have dubbed "culture" as it operates in an ethnicity regime. In the latter, among other things, culture is homogenized, in that it democratically extends to everyone what is otherwise a vast network of heterogeneous rights. Under an ethnicity regime, one can say that every Kayapó partakes in Kayapó "culture"; under the former regime—which as we will see, now coexists with the other—every Kayapó had only so many rights over so many elements of her or his culture.

Present-day Kayapó participate in both an internal order where everyone is different, and in other orders, one of which has them all subsumed as a collective and unique ethnic group vis-à-vis other ethnic groups. On still another level, they are conjoined with every other native Brazilian society as "Indians"—"generic Indians" to use Darcy Ribeiro's expression with a new twist. Each one of the three orders makes distinctions in specific ways. The issue we want to address, however, is how all these nested orders affect each other to the point they cannot be separately thought.

That this is the case is warranted by two potentially trivial remarks. One is that all these "orders" coalesce in the same human beings whose agency is implicated and mobilized in their actualization and in their future. As much as each sphere can be seen as organized by a *sui generis* logic, the same people are nevertheless simultaneously living in these multiple spheres. That implies coming to terms with the simultaneous demands implied by each one of these sphere's logics.

Then there is what Ian Hacking called the looping effect, namely that what he calls human kinds (as contrasted as well as patterned in opposition to "animal kinds") comprise beings that are aware of how they are classified, and that such awareness has effects of its own. Labeling theory holds that people institutionally branded will start to behave as they are stereotypically expected to. Ian Hacking argues, however, this is too simple an account. In the process, awareness produces in individuals behavioral changes that might actually be quite different from what is expected from the human kind in question. Thus, the kind itself becomes different, and "because the kind changes, there is new knowledge to be had about the kind. But that new knowledge in turn becomes part of what is to be known about members of the kind, who change again. This is what I call the looping effect for human kinds."

Note the parallel between the self-reflection implied in Ian Hacking's discussion and the reflexive move implied in "culture" as meta-discourse on culture. What I want to suggest here is that reflexivity has dynamic effects both on what is reflected upon: culture, and for the meta categories themselves, "culture."

The episode with which I started this pamphlet can be understood in the light of such a co-existence of culture and "culture." Recall the old Yawanawa leader protesting that *honi* (*ayahuasca*) was not *cultura*. "Culture" by definition is shared. When retranslated into vernacular terms it assumes a collective regime imposed on what previously was a network of differential rights. There is thus a collectivizing effect to the use of "culture." Everyone has it, and everyone is supposed to share in it. This, I offer, was what the old Yawanawa was objecting to. Although *honi* is available to any adult, some people have special rights linked to it, such as rights to preparing the brew. If *honi* were "cultura," the man reasoned, then everyone would claim the same rights. That such an inference could be made by this man is predicated on the co-existence of "culture" and culture.

Regimes of Knowledge

What does knowledge consist of; what falls under that category, what are its sub-divisions, its branches, its specialties? What is it a part of; what subsumes it? How is it produced? To whom is it attributed? How is it validated? How does it circulate; how is it transmitted? What rights and what duties does it generate? Responses to these and many other associated questions are highly variable, and each set of responses accounts for a sui generis knowledge regime. Our own present-day regime has been deliberately and painstakingly construed since the seventeenth century, through covenants over protocols for proof, authorship, validation, and so on.

    Almost by definition, international instruments —even with the best of intentions—fall into some traps. For a start, they do not look into the myriad variations in specific regimes of knowledge but refer to traditional knowledge as a highly homogenous notion. Traditional knowledge will be assumed to be collective, sometimes "holistic," a term whose fuzziness conveniently allows for different interpretations. Further, international instruments often seem to treat traditional knowledge as a thesaurus. That is, it is treated as a complete and closed set of facts, lore or wisdom handed down from times immemorial—to which present generations do not contribute.

That traditional knowledge is not simply a stable corpus of ancient origin, but rather an enduring set of particular forms for generating knowledge, is by now more or less established in the juridical literature and in the declarations of international indigenous movements. Traditional knowledge is not necessarily ancient. What is traditional is the procedure—its form rather than its referent.

These procedures are highly diverse. Truth criteria and research protocols in traditional knowledge regimes do not rely solely on experimentation and empirical observation, though these are no doubt passionately undertaken. As Lévi-Strauss showed in *The Savage Mind* for traditional knowledge and as Kuhn demonstrated to be at work in Western science, they also rely on what one could call logical consistency. Some things can go together in a system, others just cannot and that is something that empirical data *per se* is helpless in destabilizing. Marc Bloch, for one, gave a brilliant example of how the very category of experimental data hinges on premises: the "royal miracle" that attributed to French and English kings the power to heal scrofula was conceived of as experiential fact. When this was questioned in Renaissance Italy, the facts themselves were not disputed: rather the interest was in explaining them away or in challenging that this privilege would be exclusive to the Kings of France and England.

Sources and grounds for authoritative statements are also quite diverse. Without exhausting all their possible forms, two can be contrasted right away. Authority can be conferred to direct experience, but authority can also lie in the source itself, with every source deriving its truth-value from the succession of authoritative relays in the transmission chain of knowledge. The contrast between these two forms of authority stands out in the anecdote Marshall Sahlins likes to tell: that of a well-known humorist of the early eighteenth-century that Sir Joseph Banks, sailing in the first of captain Cook's expedition, adopted: "Since you tell me so, I am bound to believe you. But I must confess that, had I seen it with my own eyes, I would have doubted it exceedingly."

Knowledge in Melanesia, we are told by Lindstrom, is grounded in the authority of the source. According to many authors, it is instead direct experience that prevails in the Amazon. Authority attributed to elders or to shamans is thought to follow from the many things they have seen, heard and experienced. Their knowledge comes from seeing and being seen— the weight of their visual and hearing experiences. In the same vein the unlucky *panema* hunter is one who does not see, who goes into the forest without discerning the beings that inhabit it. His want is not in his hunting skills, for he does not ordinarily miss his target: he just cannot see it nor hear it. The hunter has to surpass his game in seeing it before he is seen, in hearing it before he is heard. Intimacy with the forest and its inhabitants, expertise in hunting is related to perception. One learns through direct experience, and that assumption holds for hunters and for shamans as well as much as for anyone else. In that respect, hunting stories told by the

Runa, (a Quichua-speaking Amazonian society in Ecuador) and strikingly rendered and analyzed by Eduardo Kohn, are quite instructive. They amount to perceptual memos. One endeavors to recreate for the auditor's benefit not a series of episodes, but rather a visual and auditive transcript of the experience.

David Kopenawa, a Yanomami leader whose memoirs are being elicited and transcribed by his old friend, the anthropologist Bruce Albert, often declares that to become a shaman, the *xapiripë* spirits have to see you. Reciprocally, one has to learn to see them oneself, and Kopenawa explicitly links hunting to visual and auditive perception.

> I slowly started seeing the xapiripë, for I grew up playing in the forest. I was always on the look out for game. So, at night, when I dreamt, I started really distinguishing the image of the ancestral animals as they approached me. Their ornaments and their body paintings were increasingly glowing in the dark. I could hear them speak, hear them yell.

Yet perception is anything but univocal. Hallucinogenic drugs provide direct experience of how differently one can perceive the world, or to put it in Amazonian terms how different worlds can co-exist and be perceived. As Eduardo Viveiros de Castro has suggested, Amazonian societies' ontologies are such that not everyone perceives the same things, and conversely things are perceived differently by different sentient beings. That which appears to us as a rotting cadaver is, from the vultures' point of view, an inviting beer. And what we perceive as a human being is, for the jaguar that is devouring it, a delectable wild pig. Any perception of the real is but the result of a singular point of view, without there being any privileged position. What is universal is not a set of objects out there but rather a way of organizing them. There is no sense of a shared nature onto which idiosyncratic cultures would impose an order—culture is the universal, and nature idiosyncratic. Animals and us humans organize the world in the same manner, but our referents are different from theirs. Referents of perception are species-relative but the organization—culture—is universal.

Paradoxically, perception is at once equivocal in what it stands for, and at the same time the ultimate source of knowledge. While there is, as Merleau-Ponty would put it, a primacy of perception, there is no universal agreement on its referents. Maybe this is why individual dreams, made of perceptions without references, are perfectly legitimate sources of knowledge in most Amazonian societies.

I have discussed here some procedures of validation, as an example of how the multiple dimensions that define a regime of knowledge should be interrogated.

Our Own Regime of Knowledge

In the same way that we have failed to explore the multiple regimes of traditional knowledge, our own assumptions, as basic as they are in the Western system of Intellectual property, are equally inexplicit. The current construction of intellectual property rights has, at its basis, a "romantic" notion of the creative author who builds *ab nihilo* an original oeuvre. This construct has been aptly criticized in the last few decades by people like Woodmansee, Jaszi, Rose, Boyle, Coombe, Lessig, and Adrian Johns among others. They had predecessors in the 1940s with anthropologists Kroeber and Leslie White. In the 1950s, several eminent scientists in the hard sciences, such as chemist Michael Polanyi and cybernetician Norbert Wiener, called into question the script of the creative genius. The same fallacy applies equally well to artistic creation and scientific invention. Such a demiurgic concept of authorship, as descending through an almost mystical inspiration, elides the collective and individual intellectual input on which invention and creation rest. The most notable exception, one that is hard to account for, is financial input. The institution that supports the researcher has proprietary rights. Patents are normally not the property of the individual researcher, but of the institution or corporation for which the researcher is working. As Veblen remarked long ago, this is a paradoxical extension of the reasoning behind intellectual property rights (IPR). What is paradoxical here is not that Universities or corporations would try to recoup their investment in research through IPR, but that IPR is predicated on a story of the creative genius that hardly seems compatible with attributing property to its employer or sponsor.

In actual fact, since their inception in early seventeenth-century Great Britain, authorship rights (which were to be the first Western IPRs), were created not to protect authors but rather the monopoly of London stationers that was being threatened by Scottish pirate editions. Authors themselves were not, as one would think, the instigators of debates over literary creation, but rather the London publishers.

The authors were to be bestowed with literary property in order for them to be able to sell it, assuring the publishers of a monopoly—if not eternal as was previously thought, then at least *pro tempore*. Literary property or copyrights gave authors the freedom to sell their works in exclusivity to a publisher. Rather than establishing the eternal rights of creators as a moral right against disfigurement of that work, the gist of the matter was its very alienability. Hence the figure of property. To achieve this, a considerable amount of rhetoric was deployed to model literary labor on either biologic paternity, or on agricultural work, given that Locke had established the latter as paradigm for any kind of property.

"Culture" Talk, *Kastom* Talk

As for indigenous Amazonian people themselves, it seems that they endlessly now speak of "culture" (cultura). The point was most explicitly made by Terry Turner in 1991, showing how culture had become a political resource for the Brazilian Kayapo. A similar process was extensively described for Melanesia where the word *kastom* in Neo-Melanesian now has a life of its own, divorced from its derivation in the English word "custom."

While Kayapo may use a vernacular term, it seems they mostly prefer the Portuguese word for it, *cultura*.

I would like to explore this apparently trivial detail with some Krahó material. Why should the widely used *cultura* be in Portuguese, while many other items of external origin and wider circulation, such as money, are used in a Krahó translation? It is in fact remarkable how often "culture" remains untranslated in such contexts. As Jakobson has noted, no element of a vocabulary is strictly untranslatable from one language to another. For lack of something else, neologisms or the appropriation of vernacular expressions are always available. Thus not to translate, not to incorporate some words or some roots and rather to opt for loan words, is a deliberate choice. What, then, is the significance of such a choice? To use loan words is to declare their untranslatability, something that is not dictated by linguistic limitations, but by linguistic choice. This point, which at first seems tautological, is highly significant. Loan words contain meta-semantic information: they signal that, while other means could have been used for semantic communication, one has chosen to keep them explicitly linked to a context. Loan words should be understood, by convention, in a certain key—they indicate their own interpretation register.

In a remarkable doctoral dissertation presented in 2004 at the University of Chicago, Alan Durston provides a historical illustration of my assertions. Durston's dissertation—now a book titled *Pastoral Quechua*—deals with policies from colonial Peru that presided over Quechua translation of catechisms and other liturgical texts. Church Quechua varied widely from around 1530 to 1640, but a decisive move was made in the Third Lima Council in the 1570s. The first decades of evangelization chose Quechua terms for translating Christian notions. The Third Council of Lima reversed the trend. What was clearly perceived was that such a practice made it very difficult to decide who—the Church or the people—was fooling whom?

To "Christianize" rituals, cosmologies and Quechua terms was to give subject populations the tools with which they could insert Christianity into their own Inca cosmology. To avert such risks, the Council decided to abandon usage of Quechua terms and roots and solely use loan words for important Christian concepts. Words like *santo* (saint), *confesion* (confession), *alma* (soul), and above all the words for God and the Holy Spirit, were not to be translated into Quechua. What is remarkable is that the use oft loan words in this case was not a question of maintaining the original or authoritative term, which would be Aramaic, possibly Greek (of the Septuagint translation), or Latin (from the Jerome Bible). Loan words were instead taken from the missionaries' religious Province own vernacular, and as such were Spanish (or more accurately Castilian). A similar policy from early Spanish missionaries among the Tagalog in the Philippines was reported by Vincent Rafael. A strikingly similar illustration comes from Brazil. Catechisms in the Tupi-based *lingua franca* used in Brazil by Portuguese Jesuits undergo a transformation quite similar to that of Peru. At some point they dropped the religious Tupi vocabulary choice of the early decades in favor of loan words. Now, if we compare catechisms produced by the Province of Portugal with those of a Franciscan friar from France, Martin de Nantes, we find that although both were produced at about the same time and intended for Brazilian Indians, the prose and sentences are not significantly different, but loan words are. *Nossa Senhora* (Our Lady) in Portuguese becomes *La Vierge Marie* while *Espírito Santo* (the Holy Ghost) appears as *l'Esprit Saint*. This demonstrates that what is at stake is not fidelity to an ultimate original, but the assurance that a Christian register will be maintained. What is sought is power over the hermeneutic key, control of the *intentio*. What mattered for the ecclesiastic translators of the Third Lima Council, as Durston convincingly argues, was not finding an equivalent term or locution in Quechua for rendering the contents of catechisms, but avoiding heterodox appropriations of Catholic concepts, rituals and institutions. The imperative was to command the register in which the new religion would operate and be modeled.

Thus loan words are special in that they work both semantically and meta-semantically: they not only convey meaning, they also contain their own interpretative key. An example much closer to our experience could be the use of German words in philosophical jargon. True, Heidegger famously declared that philosophical thought can only exist in Greek and German and Gadamer specifically attributes this excellence to the fact that these languages have both articles and three genders rather than two. But German words, for all their vaunted philosophical abilities, are not untranslatable in other languages. To use them in their German form signals that one is moving in philosophical terrain, that the associations and the world in which they are operating should be dissociated from common usage. There is no *ersatz* to *ersatz*.

This long detour—I assure you, the last—called our attention to the significant fact that *cultura*, *kastom*, and similar words are frequently loan words. The choice of the loan word *cultura* signals that we are situated in a specific register, an inter-ethnic register, to be distinguished from that of everyday village life. That indigenous people in Brazil will use the word *cultura* indicates that the logic of each of those systems is distinct. And as *cultura* speaks of culture, as we saw earlier, *cultura* is simply the native loan word for what I called "culture."

As separate as these systems conceptually are, they are nevertheless bound to inter-organize. Surely, we are operating at different scales, each one with its organization: one is a member of a specific house in the village, a Krahó when situated next to other neighboring ethnic groups, an Indian when testifying in Congress or in a quota system at the University, traditional people when before the UN. As different as they are, these scales are not independent, but rely on the constant work of articulation. The self-image that the Brazilian State, the UN or the pharmaceutical company bestows on Indians is part of the inter-ethnic system of representations, but that system also engages the internal affairs and structure of the village. Passages of interconnection have to be created. The Krahó college of *pajés* is one such passage, an innovation no doubt, but articulated with Krahó construction of groups. We can be easily deceived: what looks traditional, *pajés*, is construed on a model of external health services. What was reserved knowledge of specialists becomes traditional knowledge that, even if one does not share in it, is still part of one's cultural patrimony. Under the guise of a same object, the very structure of production and distribution is subverted. Is this a break or is it continuity? Partisans of the hegemonic logic of power would vote for the former. Culturalists would vote for continuity. But maybe the question is misguided, and we are actually experiencing both rupture and continuity. Dialectic work permeates the different levels where the notion of "culture" comes up, and allows one to play on several boards at once.

Such work makes use of every ambiguity, of every contradiction introduced by reflexivity.

That work is happening under our very eyes. James Leach, for one, has shown how *kastom* is being retranslated by people of Rai Coast of Papua New Guinea into a vernacular version.

In a way, this is but an example of what Marshall Sahlins has been saying all along: the categories of culture are at risk in the real world, as the real world is "under no obligation to conform to them." As something that is predicated on the inter-ethnic system, "Culture" is part of that real world. Thus, when confronted with "culture," culture has to come to terms with it: and in the process, it will be subverted and reorganized. What we are talking about here is the indigenization of "culture," of "culture" in the vernacular.

Now culture's subversion could be, and in actual fact most often is, deceitful. Most cultural items will just look the same. Keeping things looking just the same is a lot of work, and a cultural dynamic, left to itself, will most likely make things look different. Change is actually manifested in the effort to stay the same.

The story does not end here. Ian Hacking's looping effect comes into play, and the motion—the reorganization that started with culture confronting "culture"—can go on indefinitely.

"Culture" and Culture Belong to Different Realms

The issue of the "invention of culture" has its own history. It is no accident that it first appeared in the late sixties in different kinds of political and academic contexts: it was developed during the ushering in of a post-colonial era in Africa, the emergence of independent states politically divided along ethnic lines, the collapse of the melting-pot ideology in the US, the rise of anthropological studies of multi-ethnic societies, and theories of proto-political engagements and resistance. Accounting for the logic of "cultures" within this context required highlighting their diacritical features, and the contrasting traits of their performance. Contrasting traits must articulate two different systems. The first is given by the larger multi-ethnic context, and is the privileged register in which difference can be made manifest. The second is the cultural set internal to each society. A previous book of mine, under the title *Negros, Estrangeiros* (*Blacks, Foreigners*) described an example of this dynamic: liberated slaves—first and second generation Yorubas in Brazil—settled "back" in coastal West Africa in the nineteenth century. While in Brazil Yoruba descendants "remained" faithful *orisa* worshipers, those who went "back" to Yoruba country settled down, mainly as staunch Catholics but with a number of Muslims among them. Muslim-led revolts in Bahia, particularly that of 1835 coming after the independence of Haiti, had spread great fear if not panic among slave-owners, and were the source of a policy of either forcible deportation or giving liberated slaves incentives to leave. The Muslim connections notwithstanding, however, to be "Brazilian" in Lagos, Whydah, Porto Novo, Abeokuta, amounted to being Catholic. I argued that in a social system where religion, or better one's set of *orisas*, was the defining characteristic of a town and a family, it was in the logic of the system for

Brazilians to choose a contrasting and exclusive religion. And exclusive it was: the Brazilians objected to any conversion of heathens by the French missionaries who, at first, had been happily surprised to find these Catholics already settled in Lagos and Porto Novo.

While this story could be used as yet another example of the invention of culture, at another level, Catholicism was not "invented." It was part of a historical experience, and was in the logic of internal culture. Needless to say, militants in the Black movement in Brazil, while praising the study on liberated slaves in nineteenth-century Brazil that constituted the first part of my book, were quite unhappy with the story of Brazilian Catholicism in West Africa. But that is precisely the issue: "invention of culture" talk is not about culture at all, it is all about "culture," that reflexive meta-discourse on culture.

What I have added here is that the coexistence of "culture" (as a resource and weapon for asserting identity, dignity, power, and other precious things vis-à-vis states or the international community) and culture (that invisible web in which we are suspended) has its own peculiar effects.

Common language, as I said earlier, prefers completeness to consistency, and allows itself to speak on anything. It moves seamlessly from culture to "culture," and takes no notice of such distinctions as those between language and metalanguage, contemporary facts and political projects. As completeness prevails over consistency, what others would call its incoherencies is of little matter. It is in such a world, rich in all its contradictions, that we are happy to live. ■

Also available from Prickly Paradigm Press:

continued